THE RICHEST MAN IN BABYLON

WITH STUDY GUIDE

Also by Randy L. Thurman:

More than a Millionaire: Your Path to Wealth, Happiness, and a Purposeful Life—Starting Now!

The All-Weather Retirement Portfolio: Your Post-Retirement Guide to a Worry-Free Income for Life

5 Steps to Finding a Financial Advisor You Can Trust: What Questions to Ask, When to Ask Them, and Why They're So Critical for a Worry-Free Retirement

One More Step: The 638 Best Quotes for Runners

Get Rich Slowly…but Surely!

THE RICHEST MAN IN BABYLON

WITH STUDY GUIDE

THE EASY-TO-READ EDITION

TIMELESS STRATEGIES FOR BUILDING WEALTH

GEORGE S. CLASON

Revised and edited by

Randy L. Thurman, CFP®, CPA/PFS

Published by

Master Key Publications,

Oklahoma City, Oklahoma

Cover design by Damonza

ISBN: 978-1-948607-07-0

With gratitude and admiration

for all those helping others with financial literacy

All profits from the sale of this book will be donated

to support financial literacy education.

Table of Contents

Table of Contents (continued)

Reader's Guide

In the early twentieth century, George S. Clason began to publish and distribute pamphlets describing simple but powerful strategies for building wealth, using parables set in ancient Babylonia. The pamphlets were widely acclaimed for the wisdom they contained, and in 1926 they were compiled into a book under the title *The Richest Man in Babylon*.

Since then, the book has become a classic in the genre of personal finance. Many of the principles it teaches have become foundational to contemporary thinking about sound strategies for establishing and expanding one's financial security. The first of these principles, now referred to as "pay yourself first," advises that anyone at any stage in life, no matter how small or large his or her income, should put the first 10%—or more—of all earnings into a personal savings or investment account before paying other expenses. That simple practice is believed to be the first and single most important step toward financial independence.

As important and successful as Clason's original book was, there was one drawback: Much of the text was difficult to understand—or, at best, it required careful reading to understand the text, which at times distracted from its valuable message. In this edition, for the first time, that text has been updated to eliminate that distraction, so today's readers can immerse themselves in the intriguing stories and get the full benefit of their life-altering lessons.

That was the initial motivation to create this new edition of George Clason's classic. Along the way, I found other ways to make the stories more enjoyable and the information more accessible...to gild the lily, as they say.

What's New in This Easy-to-Read Edition?

To enhance your experience with these wonderful stories, I've made revisions in three key areas:

1. Readability
2. Organization
3. Updates

Readability

The original version is much like the King James version of the Bible—it's hard to read and difficult to understand. Take, for example, this passage found in the Chapter 8, "The Richest Man in Babylon," the story that gives this book its name:

> "Provide also that thy family may not want should the gods call thee to their realms. For such protection it is always possible to make provision with small payments at regular intervals. Therefore the provident man delays not in expectation of a large sum becoming available for such a wise purpose."

Here's the same passage in this new easy-to-understand edition:

> "Provide for your family so they will not be left wanting when you leave this world. It is always possible to arrange for such protection by making small payments at regular intervals. Therefore, a wise man acts accordingly and doesn't wait."

See how much easier it is to read and understand?

Organization

Little is known about the process of combining George Clason's pamphlets to create the chapters of his book, the original *The Richest Man in Babylon*. But it's difficult to discern a strategy in the arrangement of chapters in that first version. Characters appear and reappear in illogical order, and a history of the great city of Babylon comes near the end, after we've spent many chapters roaming its streets and the desert beyond. The lessons in each chapter are sound, to be sure, but the illogical arrangement creates questions, confusion, and, again, distraction. I eliminated this problem by reorganizing chapters to introduce you to beautiful Babylon at the outset, and so that characters emerge in a sequence that enhances the lessons they have to teach.

Updates

A great deal has been learned about the ancient city of Babylon since George Clason published his book in 1926. In this edition, Chapter 1, "The History of Babylon," has been revised and updated to share those new findings with you.

In the Foreword of this edition, George S. Clason speaks directly to you, his reader, as he did in his original edition of *The Richest Man in Babylon*, with inspiring words about the value of following the principles contained in his stories, and encouragement to follow their teachings closely. In the closing pages of this edition, we come full circle with an Epilog drawn from Clason's 1937 publication, *Gold Ahead: A Saga for Practical Treasure Hunters*, in which he shares his vision for his own future. In the text of a very personal monolog, reprinted here, he invites you to join him in imagining a future in which you create the realities that will bring meaning and happiness to your life. I join him now in welcoming you into a future that's abundant with financial success and personal fulfillment.

How to Get the Most Value out of This Book

[*Adapted from "Conclusion" by E. McPherson Cole*
in Gold Ahead: A Saga for Practical Treasure Hunters
by George S. Clason]

At the age of 23, I completed my master's degree in business administration with the belief that my studying days were over, that the knowledge I already had would guide me in practical ways throughout the coming years of my life. I wonder if most young people have that expectation. It's a nice idea, but doesn't work—at 23 or at any other time in your life. I've come to believe that the key to advancement is a lifelong commitment to studying and learning. We can stand on the shoulders of those thinkers and students who came before us, and see further than if we stand solely on our own experience. There is so much to learn!

I recommend to every person who wants to be financially independent to carefully study the tales in *The Richest Man in Babylon* (RMIB). To you, I suggest the following study plan:

First, read the book in its entirety. That will give you a 20,000-foot view of the material.

Then, make a more focused study of each tale in its turn. Devote a week to each one. In the course of the week read the chapter not less than three times; once a day is even better. Ponder it every day, thinking about how it applies to your life. See how it might have been applied in your past, and how you might have handled past events and decisions differently. If you see things you now wish you'd handled differently, don't let it discourage you. Use your past as a school, not an anchor.[1] Think about how the lessons in this book might apply to a friend's situation. You will be surprised at how soon you'll be able to analyze and understand situations that are similar to the stories in this book. In areas where you were once unsure what to do, you will now be confident. You will stop being a money experimenter and begin to look at money issues with a more analytical eye—and the ability to anticipate the obvious or probable results of certain actions.

Every week, focus on a new chapter in the same way. Keep in mind that by remembering the lessons in each story and evaluating

[1] Inspired by Jim Rohn, author of *The Power of Ambition: Awakening the Powerful Force Within You*.

your financial decisions accordingly, you are preparing yourself to do well with your money and handle it successfully.

Your first careful, chapter-by-chapter study of RMIB is only the beginning. Take this wisdom and embrace it, with the goal of applying it skillfully and automatically to every money-related decision you make. Soon you'll begin to develop sound habits and a practical understanding of how valuable these lessons are.

Next, mark your calendar with a plan to review the book every three months for a year, then annually thereafter. You will be surprised, when you review it in this way, how much additional knowledge and inspiration it offers. Every year you'll bring new life experience to the reading and discover wisdom you hadn't seen before. And you'll find that the more you learn, the more there is to learn.

Plan to make an annual review of RMIB a lifelong habit. That way, you'll keep these essential principles at the ready in your thoughts as your financial circumstances change and your knowledge and experience grow.

A great way to deepen your understanding of these principles is to create a study group. Plan to meet on a regular basis—weekly is ideal—and allow two meetings for the study of each chapter. In the first of those, read the tale out loud, then have each student share his or her thoughts, including what made the biggest impression. After that, allow time for members to describe specific situations, either real or hypothetical, and discuss them as a group, exploring how the lessons in RMIB would apply. For the second meeting, invite students to bring examples of real-life situations that are related to the chapter at hand. Have the group discuss how Clason's teachers would have liked to see them handled.

Finally, the best strategy of all is to work through the Study Guide that begins on page 151 of this book. It will enable you to get the maximum benefit from the wisdom in these stories—and the power they have to change your life. Study each lesson, answer each question, and keep a written record of your work that you can revisit every year. Whether you use the Study Guide on your own or with a study group you create, it will provide a step-by-step guide to a true understanding of the RMIB road to financial success, and to incorporating it into your own life so you, too, can become wealthy.

Many students have valuable results even after their first reading of Clason's stories. They take what they have learned and immediately use it. It's as though they suddenly have an age-old mastermind guiding them on how to handle a current situation. It is extremely gratifying when this happens. But it pales in comparison to the greater lifetime value that's to come. If you master these lessons and make them a part of your life, you will, for the rest of your life, be able to use this knowledge to make your life better in many ways.

–Randy L. Thurman, 2022

Foreword

by George S. Clason

Our prosperity as a nation depends upon the personal financial prosperity of each of us as individuals.

This book deals with the personal success of each of us. Success means accomplishments as the result of our own efforts and abilities. Proper preparation is the key to our success. Our acts can be no wiser than our thoughts. Our thinking can be no wiser than our understanding.

This book of cures for lean purses has been termed as a guide to financial understanding. That, indeed, is its purpose: to offer those who are ambitious for financial success an insight that will aid them in acquiring money, in keeping money, and in making their surpluses earn more money.

In the pages that follow, we are taken back to Babylon, the cradle in which was nurtured the basic principles of finance now recognized and used the world over. To new readers the author is happy to extend the wish that these pages may contain for them the same inspiration for growing bank accounts, greater financial successes, and the resolution of difficult personal financial problems so enthusiastically reported by readers from coast to coast.

To the business executives who have distributed these tales in such generous quantities to friends, relatives, employees, and associates, the author takes this opportunity to express his gratitude. No endorsement could be higher than that of practical men who appreciate its teaching because they, themselves, have worked up to important successes by applying the very principles it advocates.

Babylon became the wealthiest city of the ancient world because its citizens were the richest people of their time. They appreciated the value of money. They practiced sound financial principles in acquiring money, keeping money, and making their money earn more money. They provided for themselves what we all desire...income for the future.

–George S. Clason

Introduction

A Historical Sketch of Babylon

Arguably the most glamorous city in history was Babylon, located in the area we now know as Iraq, about fifty miles south of the modern-day city of Baghdad. The region was called Mesopotamia then, and there, more than 4,000 years ago, Babylon grew from a small village on the Euphrates River to become one of the largest, most opulent cities in the world. Even now it conjures visions of wealth and splendor. Imagine it, a city with almost an endless supply of gold and treasures.

Now, you might think a city with this much wealth would be surrounded by many natural resources to draw from—perhaps mines to tap for gold and diamonds, or forests for all the lumber they could yield. It must have been next to a natural trade route, you might assume, or have abundant annual rainfall for raising crops. But no. Babylon had none of these. It began as little more than a humble port beside a river in a flat, arid valley.

And yet Babylon flourished. It serves as an outstanding example of man's ability to overcome obstacles and achieve great objectives.

What did Babylon look like? It was organized like a modern city. There were streets and shops and peddlers offering their wares. There were magnificent churches. An inner enclosure within the city contained the royal palaces with walls even higher than the towering walls that surrounded the city.

The Walls of Babylon

The immense walls surrounding the city of Babylon were a marvel of achievement. Historians rank these walls on a par with the Great Pyramid of Giza and the other wonders of the ancient world. They were initially built around the 18th century BC, probably by a chieftain named Sumu-la-El. Herodotus, a prolific Greek writer and geographer who lived during the fifth century BC, wrote extensively about Babylon and its walls. Remarkably, in the early 20th century those walls were discovered and unearthed, largely intact, by a team of German archeologists.[2]

Even more famous were the walls that came later, as a project started by King Nabopolasser around 600 BC. He built not one, but three walls around the city, at a height of forty feet, and wide enough to conduct chariot races on top of them[3]. Against the walls were 250 guard towers that could be armed with archers and soldiers to defend against any invaders.

The project was so huge that the king did not live to see its completion. He left the task to his oldest son, Nebuchadnezzar.

---

[2] For more information, visit "Walls of Babylon," *Ancient Mesopotamia*, https://ancientmesopotamia.org/structures/walls-of-babylon.php.
[3] "Walls of Babylon," *Ancient Mesopotamia*, https://ancientmesopotamia.org/structures/walls-of-babylon.php, accessed December 21, 2021.

Water and Agriculture

Babylon did have two natural resources—the water in the river and fertile soil. In one of the impressive accomplishments of the day, or any day, engineers used dams and an intricate canal system to divert the river. Some canals were said to be wide enough to ride 12 horses through them. These canals carried the life-giving waters of the Euphrates across the arid valley to irrigate the fertile soil. Because of this, Babylonians grew a surplus of crops greater than any seen before.

There were other projects that were similarly impressive. For example, they put in an elaborate drainage system to reclaim large swaths of swampland at the mouths of the Euphrates and Tigris Rivers, and then cultivated the land.

Arts and Metal

The Babylonians were also skilled artists and metal workers. There were sculptors, painters, and weavers, and artisans who crafted gold into jewelry and other ornamental objects. Their jewelry was well known for its beauty and intricate design, and people came from far and wide to buy it...all without the home shopping network. Samples have been recovered and are, to this day, exhibited in museums around the world.

When the rest of the world was still hacking at trees with stone-headed axes and hunting or fighting with flint spears and arrows, Babylonians were using metal in their axes, spears, arrows, and agricultural equipment.

Finance and written record

The Babylonians were also wise financiers and traders. From what we can tell, they are the first in recorded history to use easily transported money, promissory notes, and written property titles. This suggests they may also have been the first society to have attorneys. Some may argue whether this is a benefit. But having a legal system for overseeing transactions, and an opportunity for recourse for citizens who were harmed, had to be good for their individual prosperity as well as the economy overall.

Attacks, Attempts to Plunder

Most kings of that era were warlike, often engaged in the conquest and plunder of other empires. The kings that ruled Babylon were different. It's true that they engaged in many wars, but most of those were in defense against attacks from other countries whose leaders coveted Babylon's riches. History remembers these kings not only because they successfully repelled invaders for centuries, but also because of their wisdom, justice, and enterprise.

Many conquering armies, victorious elsewhere, marched against Babylon and its mighty walls. Invading armies of that day were huge. Historians speak of armies with 10,000 horseman, 25,000 chariots and 1,200,000 foot soldiers. Not your normal overnight guests. Two to three years of preparation were often needed for planning and to gather war materials and stockpilearch enough food supplies for the campaign. And yet, despite all that preparation, every would-be conqueror who tried to breech the walls of Babylon failed.

The Fall of Babylon

Hostile armies never entered Babylon until 540 years before the birth of Christ—but even then, it wasn't because they managed to penetrate those famous walls. Babylon's fall is a classic story. Cyrus, one of the great conquerors of that period, led the attacking army. He intended to attack the city and its impregnable walls, just as so many others had tried to do. But he couldn't do it. He laid siege to Babylon, but the city had stored up enough food for years inside the wall, in anticipation of just such an occasion. As one story goes, Cyrus called Nabonidus, the king of Babylon at the time, a coward for hiding behind his walls, and challenged him to come out and fight like a man. As has happened to many men in positions of power, Nabonidus' ego—and the questionable counsel of his advisors—apparently overrode his good sense. He exited the protection of the walls intending to put Cyrus in his place. It proved to be a catastrophic mistake. Cyrus so resoundingly defeated the Babylon army that its soldiers fled from the city. Cyrus then entered the city's open gates and took possession without resistance.

After Cyrus' conquest, the power and prestige of this once great city gradually faded until, over the course of a few centuries, it was abandoned, and left to the winds and desert storms. Babylon had fallen, never to rise again.

Babylon as We Know It Today

Babylon no longer exists. When those engineering marvels that helped it flourish for thousands of years were removed, it soon become a ghost city.

The legendary city was set at about thirty degrees above the equator, about the same latitude as Yuma, Arizona, and shared the same climate: hot and dry. The area that was once lush, irrigated farmland is now a windswept, arid wasteland of wind-blown sands with scant grass, dotted with desert shrubs. The fertile fields, large cities, and long caravans are gone. The only inhabitants are nomads, living in tents, tending small herds.

For nearly twenty centuries, from the fall of Babylon to the early twentieth century, the exact location of the city was unknown. Archeologists knew only that it was hidden somewhere in a valley in what was once Mesopotamia, among the earthen hills. But the great city was not destined to remain hidden forever. Rainstorms occasionally washed down broken pieces of pottery and bricks, and modern archeologist took note, wondering where the treasures had come from. Eventually, a collaboration of European and American museums financed an expedition and, soon after, excavation of those hills and valleys began. The archeologists found many cities, and Babylon was one.

The now famous walls of Babylon, originally made of brick, had all but disintegrated and returned to the earth. The irrigation canals that were once a wonder of the world were located and traced, though they are now filled with sand. How sad it would have been if these wonders had never been discovered; then again, I suppose we wouldn't have known what was lost. Today, all that is left are those canals, portions of the foundations of those magnificent walls, and the moat. Not surprisingly, the elements have ravaged the structures. Sadly, local residents have also carried away remaining bricks to use them elsewhere.

Many scientists believe Babylon and other cities in the valley to be the oldest on record. It's believed that Babylon was founded around 4,000 BC, but other cities in the area have been dated to more than 8,000 years ago, or around 6,000 BC. How do they know? Modern archeologists have many ways to analyze ancient artifacts, but one is derived from the written records found in the area. Among the ruins were records of a solar eclipse. By analyzing when such an eclipse might have been visible in those hills around Babylon, they determined that those records were likely made eight millennia ago.

We can now say with certainty that as long as 8,000 years ago, Sumerians, who were among the people who resided in Babylon, lived within elaborate walled cities in the area. They were not barbarians, but educated and enlightened people. Historical records tell us they were the first engineers, the first astronomers, the first mathematicians, the first financiers, and the first to have a written language.

Its Wisdom Endures

Babylon's glory has faded, but not its wisdom, and we can learn about it because of the records its residents kept. That's quite a marvel when you consider that paper had not yet been invented. Instead, their writing, including the city's history, was engraved on moist clay tablets, which were then fired to become hardened tiles. The tablets were about six inches high and eight inches wide, and about an inch thick. Google them—they're quite impressive.

The writing on these tablets is in cuneiform script, which was developed by the Sumerians between 3,000 and 4,000 BC and is believed to be the oldest form of writing in the world. Libraries have been uncovered containing hundreds of thousands of these tablets. They contain a wealth of information about Babylonian culture, politics, government, and much more. There are lengthy legends, poetry, historical records, royal decrees, laws, titles to property, promissory notes, and more.

We gain some interesting insights from these tablets about the personal affairs of the people, such as letters that were delivered by messenger. There are even grocery lists. (That had to be a big disappointment for the archeologist hoping to find something cool.) For example, one tablet has a transaction from a store owner exchanging a cow for seven sacks of wheat, three to be delivered immediately and the others at the customer's pleasure. Another tablet shares the autobiography of one of its kings, Ashurbanipal. In it he tells us, "The beautiful writing in Sumerian, that is difficult to remember, was my joy to repeat. I directed the weaving of reed shields and breastworks like a pioneer. I had the leaning that all clerks of every kind possess when their time of maturity comes. At the same time, I learned what is proper for lordship."

It's clear that, although Babylon and its proud walls have not withstood the test of time, its wisdom endures.

CHAPTER ONE

The Walls of Babylon

Banzar may have been old, but he wasn't feeble. A retired warrior, he stood guard at the passageway leading to the top of the ancient walls of Babylon. Up above, valiant defenders were battling to hold the walls. The future existence of this great city, with its hundreds of thousands of citizens, depended on them.

Over the wall came the roar of the attacking armies, the yelling of many men, the trampling of thousands of horses.

In the street behind the gate, the spearmen were ready, waiting to defend the entrance should the gates give way. These men were brave, but their numbers were few. Their mighty king, Shamash-shum-ukin, had taken Babylon's main armies far away to Elam to wage a battle there. No attack on their beautiful city had been anticipated, so only a small force had remained behind. Unexpectedly, the mighty Assyrian army had attacked, determined to seize the great city, claim its wealth, and enslave its people.

The stakes could not be higher: If the walls were conquered, the city would be as well.

The defenders, holding their place at the top of the wall, fought off Assyrians trying to scale the wall with ladders and climbing platforms. The fierce Babylonian soldiers used arrows, burning oil, and finally spears on any attackers who reached the top.

For three days the enemy's archers circled the city and shot thousands of arrows at the wall's defenders. When that effort failed, the Assyrian army turned its strength against the weakest part of Babylon's great wall—the massive gate. It was a crucial moment in the attack. As the deafening BOOM BOOM BOOM of the battering rams pounded against the gate, the great walls of Babylon trembled—and so did the Babylonians hiding inside.

Beyond the thunder of the battering ram, the citizens could hear the attacking army's roar. The shouting of the men and the hoofbeats and snorting of thousands of horses filled the air. The Assyrian attack was brutal. As each dead or wounded defender of Babylon was carried out of the passageway, the citizens' fears grew. And grew. And grew. White faced and terrified, they sought news of the battle.

Old Banzar was closest to the battle, and the first to know of each wave of the attack and each repulse. Crowds of citizens surrounded him. An elderly gentleman pulled at the old warrior's clothes with quivering, palsied hands, and pleaded, "Tell me what is happening! The enemy must not get in. My sons are with King Shamash-shum-ukin, and there is nobody to protect my wife. They will steal my gold, my food...everything, and leave nothing. I am old, too old to defend myself—too old to be a slave. We will starve and die. Please tell me they cannot get in!"

"Calm yourself, good merchant," Banzar responded. "The walls of Babylon are strong. Go back to the bazaar and tell your wife the walls will protect you and all your possessions as safely as they protect the rich treasures of the king. Keep close to the walls, so the arrows flying over them will not strike you."

A small child tugged on Banzar's belt. "Tell me please, sir, what is happening?" She cried with fear. "I hear the awful noises. I see the men are all bleeding. I am afraid. What will happen to our family, to my mother? Will my little brother and the baby be taken away?"

The grim old soldier blinked his eyes and thrust his chin forward as he gazed upon the child. "Be not afraid, little one," he reassured her. "The walls of Babylon will protect you and your mother and little brother and the baby. It was for the safety of citizens like you that the good chieftain Sumu-la-El built them more than a hundred years ago. No enemy has ever broken through them, nor will this one. Go back and tell your family the walls will protect them. They have nothing to fear."

Day after day, old Banzar stood at his post and watched soldiers, some dead, some injured, carried through the passageway. And day after day he saw reinforcements go up to the top of the wall to fight until they returned, wounded or dead. Around him, throngs of frightened citizens crowded day and night, eagerly seeking to learn if the walls would hold. To all he gave his answer with the fine dignity of an old soldier. Again and again he assured them, "The walls of Babylon will protect you."

For weeks the attack continued, and the violence took a terrible toll. The blood of wounded and dying men turned the hard-packed dirt of the passageway to mud, churned up by the unending flow of defenders staggering down from the wall and replacements climbing up. Each day, the bodies of slaughtered attackers piled up in heaps on the far side of the wall, and each night their fellow soldiers carried them away and buried them.

As Banzar watched it all unfold, the set of his jaw grew more stern and his gaze more grim. Each time his neighbors came to ask for his assessment, he replied, "Be brave! Babylon's walls will protect you and your family. They are high and strong. Take courage from our valiant defenders as they pour burning oil on our enemy!"

And then, on the fifth night of the fourth week of mayhem, when the soldiers and citizens of Babylon were exhausted with bloodshed and fear, the tumult ceased. When the first streaks of daylight illuminated the plains, they revealed great clouds of dust raised by the retreating Assyrian armies.

The defenders of the wall shouted in victory! The troops inside the wall and the citizens in the street knew the meaning of that cry, and they joined in the celebration. People rushed from their homes with wild shouts of joy. Cheering mobs jammed the streets. A victory fire was lit in the tower of the highest temple, the Temple of Bel. Its blue smoke floated high into the sky, carrying the message far and wide.

The walls of Babylon had once again held strong against a vicious and mighty foe, a foe determined to loot her rich treasures and enslave her citizens.

The great city of Babylon endured century after century because it was fully protected. It could not afford to leave such things to chance.

The walls of Babylon were an outstanding example of man's need and desire for protection. This desire is inherent in the human race. It is just as strong today as it ever was, but we have developed broader and better plans to accomplish the same purpose.

In this day, behind the impregnable walls of insurance, savings accounts, and dependable investments, we can guard ourselves against the unexpected tragedies that may enter any door and seat themselves before any fireside.

Just as the city of Babylon and its citizens needed to build those walls to protect them from disaster, each of us in this day and time need to protect ourselves from financial mayhem. The stories you'll read next will tell how those citizens might have built a safe and secure financial future for themselves. These stories are based on principles that are just as useful today as they would have been many thousands of years ago. See if you can use them to help build your own walls of financial protection.

CHAPTER TWO

The Man Who Desired Gold

Bansir, the chariot builder of Babylon, was thoroughly discouraged. He sat on the low wall surrounding his property and gazed sadly at his simple home and his open workshop, where a chariot he had been building stood unfinished.

His wife frequently appeared at the open door. Her worried glances in his direction reminded him that her grain bin was nearly empty, and he should be at work finishing the chariot—hammering and hewing, polishing and painting, stretching the leather taut over the wheel rims—and preparing it for delivery so he could collect payment from his wealthy customer.

Nevertheless, Bansir's fat, muscular body sat listlessly upon the wall. His slow mind grappled patiently with a problem, but he could not find an answer. The blazing hot sun, so typical of this valley of the Euphrates, beat down upon him mercilessly. Beads of perspiration formed on his brow and trickled down his neck.

Beyond his home, a high, terraced wall surrounded the king's palace. Nearby, the painted tower of the Temple of Bel reached far up into the blue heavens. In the shadow of such grandeur, Bansir's simple home seemed humble indeed, as did many others that were far less tidy and well cared for. Babylon was like this—a mixture of grandeur and shabbiness, of dazzling wealth and the direst poverty, all crowded together without a plan or system, within the protecting walls of the city.

Bansir could hear the noisy chariots of the rich as they surged through the streets behind his home, jostling the tradesmen in their fine sandals as well as the barefooted beggars. Even the chariots were forced to move aside into the gutters to clear the way for the long lines of slaves. They were water carriers on the "king's business," and each one carried a heavy goatskin of water to be poured upon the hanging gardens at the king's palace.

Bansir was too engrossed in his own problem to hear or heed the confused hubbub of the busy city. It was the unexpected twanging of the strings from a familiar lyre that aroused him from his reverie. He turned and looked into the sensitive, smiling face of his best friend—Kobbi, the musician.

"May the gods bless you abundantly, my good friend," began Kobbi with an elaborate salute. "But wait—it appears they have already been so generous that you do not need to work. I rejoice with you in your good fortune! Indeed, I would be honored to share in your good fortune. Surely your purse must be filled to the brim with coins, or else you would be busy working in your shop. Therefore, if you will, take just two humble copper coins from that purse and lend them to me until after the noblemen's feast tonight. I will return them to you before you miss them."

"If I did have two coppers," Bansir responded gloomily, "I would lend them to no one—not even to you, my best friend, for they would be my fortune—my entire fortune. No one lends his entire fortune, not even to his best friend."

"What?" exclaimed Kobbi with genuine surprise. "You don't have a single copper in your purse, yet you sit like a statue upon a wall? Why not finish building that chariot? How else will you pay for the goods you require to satisfy your mighty appetite? This is not like you, my friend. Where is your endless energy? Is something distressing you? Have the gods brought troubles to your doorstep?

"It must indeed be a torment from the gods," Bansir agreed. "It began with a dream, a senseless dream, in which I was a man of means. A handsome purse, heavy with coins, hung from my belt. There were coppers that I cast with careless freedom to the beggars. There were pieces of silver that I used to purchase fine garments for my wife and whatever I desired for myself. There were pieces of gold that made me confident that our future is secure, and unafraid of spending the silver. A glorious feeling of contentment was within me! You would not have recognized me as your hardworking friend. Nor would you have known my wife, with her face so free from wrinkles and shining with happiness. She was again the smiling maiden of our early married days."

"A pleasant dream, indeed," commented Kobbi. "But why should the pleasant feelings it aroused turn you into a glum statue upon the wall?"

"Why, indeed! Because when I woke up and remembered how empty my purse was, a feeling of rebellion swept over me. Let us talk it over together, my friend, for, as the sailors say, we ride in the same boat, you and I. As youngsters, we went together to the priests to learn wisdom. As young men, we shared the joys and adventures of our youth. As grown men, we have always been close friends. We have carried on, day after day, content with our lot in life. We have been satisfied to work long hours and spend our earnings freely. We have earned many coins in the years that have passed, and yet can only dream about the joys of wealth."

Bansir slapped his callused hand against the solid wall. "Bah!" he cried. "Are we not wiser than sheep? We live in the richest city in all the world. The travelers say no other city compares to it in wealth. We are surrounded by extravagant displays of wealth, but we ourselves have none of it. After half a lifetime of hard labor, you, my best of friends, have an empty purse and say to me, 'May I borrow such a trifle as two coppers until after the noblemen's feast tonight?' Then what do I reply? Do I say, 'Here is my purse; its contents I will gladly share'? No. Instead, I must admit that my purse is as empty as yours.

"What is the matter with us, Kobbi? Why are we unable to acquire silver and gold—more than just enough for the simplest food and robes?

"Consider, also, our sons," Bansir went on. "Are they not following in the footsteps of their fathers? Must they and their families and their sons and their sons' families live all their lives in the midst of such treasures of gold, and yet, like us, be content to dine upon sour goat's milk and porridge?"

Kobbi was puzzled. "Never before," he said, "in all the years of our friendship, have you spoken like this, my friend."

Bansir shook his head and responded, "Never before in all those years did I think like this. Day after day, from early dawn until the dark of night stopped me, I have labored to build the finest chariots any man could make. In my soft heart I hoped that someday the gods would recognize my worthy deeds and bless me with great prosperity. They have never done it. At last, I realize they never will. Therefore, my heart is sad. I wish to be a man of means. I wish to own lands and cattle, to wear fine robes and have coins in my purse. I am willing to work for these things with all the strength in my back, with all the skill in my hands, with all the cunning in my mind, but I wish my labors to be fairly rewarded. What is the matter with us? Again I ask you! Why can we not have our just share of the good things that are so plentiful for those who have the gold with which to buy them?"

"If only I knew the answer!" Kobbi replied. "I am no more satisfied than you. My earnings from my lyre are quickly gone. Often I must plan and scheme so that my family will not go hungry. Also, within my heart is a deep longing for a lyre large enough that it may truly sing the strains of music that surge through my mind. With such an instrument, I could make music finer than even the king has heard before."

"You should have such a lyre, Kobbi," said Bansir. "No man in all of Babylon could make it sing more sweetly, so sweetly that not only the king but the gods themselves would be delighted! But how can you have it while both of us are as poor as the king's slaves? Listen to the bell! Here they come." He pointed to the long column of half-naked, sweating water-bearers plodding laboriously up the narrow street from the river. Five abreast they marched, each bent under a heavy goatskin of water.

Kobbi gestured toward the man wearing the bell, who marched in front of the slaves, carrying no load. "He who leads them is a fine figure of a man," he said. "It is easy to see he is a prominent man in his own country."

"There are many good figures in the line," Bansir agreed, "good men, as you and I are. Tall, blond men from the north, laughing black men from the south, little brown men from the nearer countries. All march together from the river to the gardens, back and forth, day after day, year after year. They have no happiness to look forward to, only beds of straw on which to sleep and hard grain porridge to eat. Pity the poor brutes, Kobbi!"

"Pity them I do," answered his friend, "but you make me see that we are only a little better off than those slaves, even though we call ourselves free men."

"That is truth, Kobbi, as unpleasant a thought as it is. We do not wish to go on year after year living slavish lives. Working, working, working! And getting nowhere."

Kobbi was quiet for a moment. "Bansir," he inquired, "what do you think? Might we be able to find out how others acquire gold, and do as they do?"

Bansir looked at his companion. "Your question is a worthy one, my friend. Perhaps there is some secret we might learn if we simply sought it from those who know," he replied thoughtfully.

"This very day," suggested Kobbi, "I passed our old friend, Arkad, riding in his golden chariot. This I will say, he did not look over my humble head as many in his station might believe he had a right to do. Instead, he waved his hand so that all onlookers might see him offer greetings and bestow his smile of friendship upon Kobbi, the musician."

"He is claimed to be the richest man in all of Babylon," Bansir mused.

"So rich that the king is said to seek his golden aid in affairs of the treasury," Kobbi replied.

"So rich," Bansir said in a hoarse whisper, "I fear that if I should meet him in the darkness of the night, I might lay my hands upon his fat purse."

"Nonsense!" scolded Kobbi. "A man's wealth is not in the purse he carries. A fat purse quickly empties if there is no golden stream to refill it. Arkad has an income that constantly keeps his purse full, no matter how liberally he spends."

"Income—that is the thing," exclaimed Bansir. "I wish to have an income that will keep flowing into my purse whether I sit upon the wall or travel to far lands. Arkad must know how a man can make such an income for himself. Do you suppose it is something he could make clear to a mind as slow as mine?"

"I believe he taught his knowledge to his son, Nomasir," Kobbi responded. "Did he not go to Nineveh and, so it is told at the inn, become one of the richest men in that city, with no aid from his father?"

"Kobbi, you bring to me a valuable thought." A new light gleamed in Bansir's eyes. "It costs nothing to ask wise advice from a good friend, and Arkad was always that. Never mind that our purses are as empty as the falcon's nest of a year ago. Let that not deter us. We are weary of being without gold in the midst of plenty. We wish to become men of means. Come, let us go to Arkad and ask how we, too, may acquire incomes for ourselves."

"You speak with true inspiration, Bansir. You bring to my mind a new understanding. You make me realize the reason why we have never found any measure of wealth. We never sought it! You have labored patiently to build the staunchest chariots in Babylon. You devoted your best effort to that purpose. Therefore, you did succeed at it. With great effort I worked to become a skillful lyre player. And I did succeed.

"In those things toward which we applied our greatest effort, we succeeded. The gods were content to let us continue in that way. Now, at last, we see a light, one that is bright like the light of the rising sun. It bids us to learn more so that we may prosper more. With a new understanding, we shall find honorable ways to accomplish our desires."

"Let us go to Arkad this very day," Bansir urged. "Also, let us ask other friends of our boyhood days to join us, so that those who have fared no better than we have may also share in Arkad's wisdom."

Kobbi smiled warmly and said, "You were always mindful, in this way, of the needs of your friends, Bansir. Therefore you have many friends. It shall be as you say. We will take them with us and go to Arkad today."

CHAPTER THREE

THE CAMEL TRADER OF BABYLON

It is often said that the hungrier you become, the clearer your mind works—and the more sensitive you become to the smell of food.

Tarkad, the son of Azure, certainly thought so. For two whole days the young man had tasted no food except two small figs stolen from over the wall of a garden. Before he could grab a third, the angry Babylonian wife rushed forth and chased him down the street. Her shrill cries were still ringing in his ears as he walked through the marketplace. They helped him restrain his restless fingers from snatching the tempting fruits from the baskets of the market women.

Never before had he realized how much food was brought to the markets of Babylon and how good it smelled. Leaving the market, he walked across to the inn and paced back and forth in front of the café. Perhaps here he might meet someone he knew, someone from whom he could borrow a copper that would gain him a smile from the unfriendly innkeeper and, with it, a liberal helping of food. Without the copper, Tarkad knew all too well how unwelcome he would be.

While lost in his thoughts, he unexpectedly found himself face to face with the one man he wished most to avoid—tall and bony Dabasir, the camel trader. Of all the friends and others from whom he had borrowed small sums, Dabasir made Tarkad feel the most uncomfortable because of his failure to keep his promises to repay promptly.

Dabasir's face lit up at the sight of him. "Ha! It is Tarkad, just the one I have been seeking, that he might repay the two pieces of copper I loaned him a moon ago...and also the piece of silver I loaned him before that. It is good that we meet. I can make good use of the coins this very day. What do you say, boy? What do you say?"

Tarkad stuttered and his face flushed. He had nothing in his empty stomach to give him strength to argue with the outspoken Dabasir. "I am sorry, very sorry," he mumbled weakly, "but this day I have neither the copper nor the silver with which to repay you."

"Then get it!" Dabasir insisted. "Surely you can get hold of a few coppers and a piece of silver to repay the generosity of an old friend of your father who helped you when you were in need."

"I am truly sorry Dabasir, but bad luck pursues me. That is why I cannot repay you."

"Bad luck! Would you blame the gods for your own weakness? Bad luck pursues every man who thinks more of borrowing than of repaying. Come with me, boy, while I eat. I am hungry, and I would like to tell you a story."

Tarkad flinched at the brutal frankness of Dabasir, but here at least was an invitation to enter the coveted doorway of the café.

Dabasir pushed him to a far corner of the room where they seated themselves upon small rugs.

When Kauskor, the proprietor, appeared smiling, Dabasir addressed him with his usual freedom. "Fat lizard of the desert, bring me a leg of the goat, brown with plenty of juice, and bread and all of the vegetables, for I am hungry and I want a great deal of food. Do not forget my friend here. Bring him a jug of water. Have it cooled, for the day is hot."

Tarkad's heart sank. Must he sit here and drink water while he watched this man devour an entire goat leg? He said nothing. He could think of nothing to say.

Dabasir, however, knew no such thing as silence. Smiling and waving good-naturedly to the other customers, all of whom knew him, he continued. "I heard from a traveler, who just returned from Urfa, about a certain rich man who has a piece of stone cut so thin that one can look through it. He put it in the window of his house to keep out the rains. It is yellow, so this traveler says, and he was permitted to look through it. All the outside world looked strange, and not as it really is. What do you say to that, Tarkad? Do you think all the world could appear to be a different color from what it is?"

"I dare say it could," responded the youth, much more interested in the fat leg of goat placed before Dabasir.

"Well, I know it to be true, for I myself have seen the world appear to be of a different color from what it really is. The tale I am about to tell explains how I came to see it in its right color once again."

"Dabasir will tell a tale," whispered a neighboring diner to his neighbor as he dragged his rug close. Other diners brought their food and gathered around in a semi-circle. They chewed noisily in Tarkad's ears and brushed him with their meaty bones. He alone was without food. Dabasir did not offer to share with him, nor did he offer even the small corner of hard bread that had broken off and fallen from the platter to the floor.

"The tale I am about to tell," began Dabasir, pausing to bite a goodly chunk from the goat leg, "relates to my early life and how I came to be a camel trader. Did anyone know that I once was a slave in Syria?"

A murmur of surprise ran through the audience. Dabasir listened with satisfaction.

"When I was a young man," continued Dabasir after another vicious onslaught on the goat leg, "I learned the trade of my father—the making of saddles. I worked with him in his shop, and I took a wife. Being young and not greatly skilled, I could earn only a little, just enough to support my excellent wife in a modest way. I craved good things that I could not afford. Soon I found that the shopkeepers would trust me to pay later, even though I could not pay at the time.

"Being young and without experience, I did not know that he who spends more than he earns is sowing the winds of needless self-indulgence, from which he is sure to reap the whirlwinds of trouble and humiliation. So I indulged my whims for fine garments and bought luxuries for my good wife and our home, all of which were beyond our means.

"I paid as I could, and for a while all went well. But in time I discovered I could not use my earnings both to live on and to pay my debts. Creditors began to pursue me to pay for my extravagant purchases, and my life became miserable. I borrowed from my friends, but could not repay them, either. Things went from bad to worse. My wife returned to her father, and I decided to leave Babylon and seek another city where a young man might have better chances.

"For two years I had a restless and unsuccessful life working for caravan traders. From this I fell in with a set of likeable robbers, who scoured the desert for unarmed caravans. Such deeds were unworthy of the son of my father, but I was seeing the world through a colored stone and did not realize to what degradation I had fallen.

"We met with success on our first trip, capturing a rich haul of gold and silks and valuable merchandise. We took this loot to Ginir and sold it, and squandered our bounty.

"The second time we were not so fortunate. Just after we had made our capture, we were attacked by the spearmen of a native chief, whom the caravans had hired to protect them. Our two leaders were killed, and the rest of us were taken to Damascus where we were stripped of our clothing and sold as slaves.

"I was purchased for two pieces of silver by a Syrian desert chief. With my hair shorn and but a loin cloth to wear, I was not so different from the other slaves. Being a reckless youth, I thought it was merely an adventure until my master took me before his four wives and told them they could have me for a eunuch.

"Then, indeed, did I realize the hopelessness of my situation. These men of the desert were fierce and warlike. Without weapons or means of escape, I was subject to their will.

"I stood quaking in fear as those four women looked me over. I wondered if I could expect pity from them. Sira, the first wife, was older than the others. Her face was expressionless as she looked upon me. I turned away from her with little consolation. The next was the most beautiful of the four, but her eyes were filled with contempt; she gazed at me as indifferently as if I had been a lowly earthworm. The two younger ones giggled as though it were all an exciting joke.

"It seemed an age went by as I stood awaiting my sentence. Each woman appeared willing to have the others decide. Finally Sira spoke up in a cold voice.

"'We have plenty of eunuchs. But we have only a few camel tenders, and they are a worthless lot. Earlier today I wanted to visit my mother, who is sick with the fever, and there is no slave I would trust to lead my camel. Ask this slave if he can lead a camel.'

"My master then asked me, 'What do you know of camels?'

"Striving to conceal my eagerness, I replied, 'I can make them kneel, I can load them, I can lead them on long trips without tiring. If need be, I can repair their saddles and harnesses.'

"'The slave speaks up well enough,' observed my master. 'If you wish, Sira, take this man for your camel tender.'

"And so I was turned over to Sira, and that day I led her camel upon a long journey to her sick mother. I took the occasion to thank her for her intercession, and also to tell her I was not a slave by birth, but the son of a free man and an honorable saddle maker of Babylon. I also told her much of my story. Her comments were disconcerting, and I thought deeply afterword about what she said.

"'How can you call yourself a free man when your weakness has brought you to this? If a man has in himself the soul of a slave, will he not become one regardless of the status he is born to, even as water seeks its own level? If a man has within him the soul of a free man, will he not become respected and honored in his own city in spite of his misfortune?'

"For over a year I was a slave and lived with the slaves, but I could not become as one of them. One day Sira asked me, 'In the evenings when the other slaves mingle and enjoy one another's company, why do you sit in your tent alone?'

"I responded, 'I am pondering what you have said to me. I wonder if I have the soul of a slave. I cannot be like them, so I must sit alone.'

"'I, too, must sit alone,' she confided. 'My dowry was large and my lord married me because of it. Yet he does not desire me. Every woman longs to be desired. Because of this, and because I am barren and have neither a son nor a daughter, I must sit apart. If I were a man I would rather die than be a slave, but the traditions of our tribe make women into slaves.'

"'What do you think of me by this time?' I asked her suddenly. 'Have I the soul of a free man or have I the soul of a slave?'

"'Have you a desire to repay the just debts you owe in Babylon?' she asked.

"'Yes, I have the desire. But I see no way to do it.'

"'If you are content to let the years slip by and make no effort to repay, then you have but the contemptible soul of a slave. No man is anything but a slave if he cannot respect himself, and no man can respect himself if he does not repay honest debts.'

"'But what can I do, when I am nothing more than a lowly slave in Syria?'

"'Stay a slave in Syria, you weakling.'

"'I am not a weakling!' I denied hotly.

"'Then prove it.'

"'But how?'

"'Observe the lives of men you admire. Your great king fights his enemies in every way he can and with every force he has, does he not? Your debts are your enemies. They ran you out of Babylon. You left them alone and they grew too strong for you. If you had fought them as a man, you could have conquered them and been an honored man among the townspeople. But you did not have the soul to fight them, and therefore your pride has faded until you are a slave in Syria.'

"I thought day and night about her unkind accusations. I concocted many defensive phrases to prove that I was not a slave at heart, but I never had the opportunity to use them. Three days later, Sira's maid took me to her mistress.

"'My mother is again very sick,' she said. 'Saddle the two best camels in my husband's herd. Tie on water skins and saddlebags for a long journey. The maid will give you food at the kitchen tent.'

"I packed the camels, bewildered by the quantity of provisions the maid provided, for the mother lived less than a day's journey away. Nevertheless we set out, and I led the camel of my mistress while the maid rode the rear camel following behind.

"We reached Siri's mother's house just after dark. She dismissed the maid and said to me, 'Dabasir, do you have the soul of a free man or the soul of a slave?'

"'I have the soul of a free man,' I insisted.

"'Now is your chance to prove it. Your master and his chiefs have drunk themselves into a stupor. Take these camels and make your escape. Here in this bag is a garment of your master's to wear as a disguise. I will say you stole the camels and ran away while I visited my sick mother.'

"'You have the soul of a queen,' I told her. 'I wish desperately that I could lead you to happiness.'

"'Happiness,' she responded, 'does not await the runaway wife who seeks it in far lands among strange people. Go your own way, and may the gods of the desert protect you, for you have a great distance to travel with no food or water to be found along the way.'

"I needed no further urging, but thanked her warmly and headed off into the night. I did not know this strange country and had only a dim idea how to find my way from this land to Babylon, but I struck out bravely across the desert toward the hills. I rode one camel and led the other. I traveled all that night and all the next day, urged on by the knowledge of the terrible fate that would befall a slave who stole his master's property and tried to escape.

"Late that afternoon, I reached a rough country as uninhabitable as the desert. The sharp rocks bruised the feet of my faithful camels, and soon they were picking their way slowly and painfully along. I saw no other man nor beast, and could understand very well why they shunned this inhospitable land.

"From that point on it was the kind of journey few men live to tell about. Day after day we plodded along. The food and water ran out. The heat of the sun was merciless. At the end of the ninth day, I slid from the back of my mount with the feeling that I was too weak to ever remount, certain that I would die, lost in this abandoned country.

"I stretched out upon the ground and slept, not waking until the first gleam of daylight.

"I sat up and looked around me. There was a coolness in the morning air. My camels lay dejected not far away. We were surrounded by a vast waste of broken country covered with rock and sand and thorny things, with no sign of water and nothing for a man or camel to eat.

"Could it be that in this peaceful quiet I faced my end? My mind was clearer than it had ever been before. My body now seemed to be of little importance. My parched and bleeding lips, my dry and swollen tongue, and my empty stomach had all lost their terrible agonies of the day before.

"As I looked across into the uninviting distance, once again the question came to me. 'Have I the soul of a slave or the soul of a free man?' Then, with clarity, I realized that if I had the soul of a slave, I would give up, lie down in the desert, and die—a fitting end for a runaway slave.

"But if I had the soul of a free man, what then? Surely I would force myself to make my way back to Babylon, repay the people who had trusted me, bring happiness to my wife who truly loved me, and bring peace and contentment to my parents.

"'Your debts are your enemies who have run you out of Babylon,' Sira had said. It was true. Why had I refused to stand my ground like a man? Why had I permitted my wife to go back to her father?

"Then a strange thing happened. All the world seemed to be a different color, as though I had been looking at it through a colored stone that had suddenly been removed. At last I saw the true values in life.

"Die in the desert? Not I! With a new vision, I saw the things that I must do. First I would go back to Babylon and face every man to whom I owed an unpaid debt. I would tell each one that after years of wandering and misfortune, I had come back to pay my debts as fast as the gods would permit. Next I would make a home for my wife and become a citizen of whom my parents could be proud.

"My debts were my enemies, but the men I owed were my friends, for they had trusted me and believed in me.

"I staggered weakly to my feet. What did it matter if I was hungry? What did it matter if I was thirsty? Hunger and thirst were merely incidental events on the road to Babylon. Within me surged the soul of a free man going back to conquer his enemies and reward his friends. My spirits soared with my new resolve.

"The glazed eyes of my camels brightened at the new note in my husky voice. With great effort, after many attempts, they rose to their feet. With pitiful perseverance they pushed on toward the north, where something within me said we would find Babylon.

"We found water. We passed into a more fertile country where grass and fruit grew. We found the trail to Babylon because the soul of a free man looks at life as a series of problems to be solved and solves them, while the soul of a slave whines, 'What can I do when I am only a slave?'

"How about you, Tarkad? Does your empty stomach make your head exceedingly clear? Are you ready to take the road that leads back to self-respect? Can you see the world in its true color? Do you have the desire to pay your honest debts, however many they may be, and become once again a man who is respected in Babylon?"

Tears came to the eyes of the youth. He rose eagerly to his knees. "You have shown me a vision. Already I feel the soul of a free man surge within me."

An interested listener spoke up. "But, Dabasir, how did you fare upon your return to Babylon?"

"Where there is determination, the way can be found," he replied. "Once I had the determination, I set out to find the way. First I visited every man to whom I was indebted and begged for his indulgence until I could earn the coins with which to repay him. Most of them gladly agreed to my request. Several scorned me, but others offered to help me. One indeed gave me the very help I needed. It was Mathon, the gold lender. When he learned I had been a camel tender in Syria, he sent me to old Nebatur, the camel trader, who had just been hired by our good king to purchase many herds of sound camels for the great expedition. With him, I put my knowledge of camels to good use. Gradually I was able to repay every copper and every piece of silver. Then at last I could hold up my head and feel that I was an honorable man among men."

Again Dabasir turned his attention to his food. "Kauskor, you snail," he called loudly enough to be heard in the kitchen, "the food is cold. Bring me more meat, fresh from the roasting. Bring also a very large portion for Tarkad, the son of my old friend, who is hungry and shall eat with me."

So ended the tale of Dabasir the camel trader of old Babylon. He found his own soul when he realized a great truth, a truth that had been known and used by wise men long before his time.

It has led men of all ages out of difficulties and into success, and it will continue to do so for those who have the wisdom to understand its magic power. It is freely available for the use of any man who reads these lines.

WHEN YOU FIND THE DETERMINATION
TO REACH YOUR GOAL,
YOU CAN FIND THE WAY.

CHAPTER FOUR

The Luckiest Man in Babylon

Sharru Nada, the merchant prince of Babylon, rode proudly at the head of his caravan. He liked fine cloth and wore rich and becoming robes. He also liked fine animals, and sat easily on his spirited Arabian stallion. To look at him, one would hardly have guessed his advanced years. Certainly no one would have suspected that he was inwardly troubled.

The journey from Damascus is long, and the hardships of the desert are many. The Arab tribes are fierce and eager to loot rich caravans. But Sharru Nada did not fear them, for he was well protected by his many guards on their fleet horses.

Instead, it was the youth at his side, whom he was bringing to Babylon from Damascus, that troubled him. The young man was Hadan Gula, the grandson of Arad Gula, Sharru's partner of years past, to whom he felt he owed a debt of gratitude that could never be repaid. He would like to do something for this grandson, but the more he considered it, the more difficult it seemed because of the attitudes of the youth himself.

Eyeing the young man's rings and earrings and embroidered garments, Sharru thought to himself, "He believes jewelry is for men of stature, and wears gaudy robes unlike the simple garments his grandfather wore. Still, he has his grandfather's strong face. I sought him out and invited him to come with me, hoping I might help him get a good start for himself, away from the habits of excess that had led his father to squander their inheritance."

Hadan Gula interrupted Sharru's thoughts. "Why do you work so hard, always riding with your caravan on its long journey? Do you never take time to enjoy life?"

Sharru smiled. "To enjoy life?" he repeated. "What would you do to enjoy life if you were Sharru Nada?"

"If I had your wealth I would live like a prince. I would never ride across the hot desert. I would spend my coins as fast as they came into my purse. I would wear the richest of robes and the rarest of jewels. That would be a life to my liking, a life worth living!"

Both men laughed.

"Your grandfather wore no jewels." Sharru had spoken before he thought. To ease the moment, he continued jokingly, "Would you leave no time for work?"

"Work was made for slaves," Hadan responded.

Sharru bit his lip but said nothing. Together they rode in silence until they came to a slope, where Sharru stopped and pointed at the green valley far away.

"See, there is the valley," he said. "If you look to the far end, you can faintly see the walls of Babylon. That tower is the Temple of Bel.

If your eyes are sharp enough, you might even see the smoke from the eternal fire at the top of the temple."

"So that is Babylon? I have always longed to see the wealthiest city in all the world," Haden commented. "Babylon, where my grandfather built his fortune. I wish he were still alive, then we would not need to struggle as we do now."

"Why wish his spirit to linger on earth beyond its allotted time? You and your father can carry on his good work."

"If only that were true. Alas, neither of us has my grandfather's gift. Neither Father nor I know his secret for attracting gold."

Sharru Nada did not reply, but loosened the reins on his horse and rode, lost in thought, down the trail to the valley. The caravan followed behind, stirring up a cloud of red dust.

In time they reached the king's highway and turned south through the irrigated farmlands, where Sharru's attention was drawn to three elderly men plowing a field. They seemed strangely familiar. "How odd," he thought. "One does not come back after forty years and find the same men plowing a field." Still, something told him these were the same men he'd seen before. One had an uncertain grip on the plow. The others trudged along beside the oxen, with a halfhearted effort at prodding the beasts to keep them pulling the plow.

Forty years ago Sharru had envied these men! How gladly he would have exchanged places with them! At that time his life was not his own, and his destiny seemed to be in the hands of others. But his life was so different now. He looked back with pride at his trailing caravan of well-chosen camels and mules loaded high with valuable goods from Damascus. All of this was but a small portion of his possessions.

He pointed to the men plowing and said, "Look at those men, Hadan, still plowing the same field, just as they were forty years ago."

"Why do you think they are the same men?"

"I saw them there," Sharru replied.

Memories came flooding back. Why could he not bury the past and live in the present? Then in his minds eye he saw, as in a picture, the smiling face of Arad Gula. In an instant, the barrier he had sensed between himself and the cynical young man beside him crumbled.

But how could he help Hadan, this youth with his superior attitude, his extravagant habits, and his bejeweled hands? He could easily offer plenty of work to men who were willing to apply themselves, but that was of little use to one who considered himself too good for work. And yet, he owed it to Arad Gula to do something for this lad, and a half-hearted attempt would never do. He and Arad had never done things that way. They were not that sort of men.

Suddenly a plan came to mind. It was not without complication. He had his own family to consider, and his own standing. It would be cruel, and it would hurt. But he was a decisive man, and he waived aside his reservations and acted.

"Would you be interested in hearing how your worthy grandfather and I joined in the partnership that became so profitable?" he questioned.

"Why not just tell me what you did to acquire the gold? That is all I need to know," the young man responded.

Sharru Nada ignored the reply and continued. "The story begins with those men plowing the field. I was no older than you the first time I saw them. I was marching past them in a column of men, on our way to Babylon. Megiddo, a good old farmer, was chained next to me. As we approached the men in the field, Megiddo scoffed, 'Look at those lazy fellows. The plow holder makes no effort to plow deep, and the ox handlers don't keep the oxen in the furrow. How can they expect to raise a good crop with poor plowing?'"

Hadan looked startled. "Did I hear you right?" he asked. "Did you say the old farmer was chained to you?"

"Yes, with bronze collars around our necks and a length of heavy chain between us. Next to him was Zabado, a sheep thief. I had known him in Harroun. At the end was a man we called 'Pirate,' because he never told us his name. We assumed he was a sailor, since he had entwined serpents tattooed on his chest, as sailors often do. We were chained together in this way, as were all the men in the column, so we could walk in fours."

"You were chained as a slave?" Hadan asked, incredulous.

"Did your grandfather not tell you I was once a slave?"

"He often spoke of you, but never hinted at that."

"Yes, he was a man you could trust with your innermost secrets. You are also a man I may trust, are you not?" Sharru Nada looked Hadan Gula straight in the eye.

"You may rely on my silence, but I am amazed. Tell me, how did you come to be a slave?"

Sharru shrugged his shoulders. "Any man may find himself a slave. It was a gaming house and barley beer that brought me disaster. I was the victim of my brother's indiscretions. In a brawl, he killed a friend to whom he owed gambling debts. My father was desperate to keep my brother out of prison, so he assigned me to the friend's widow against a pledge to pay the debts. When my father could not raise the gold to release me, the widow was infuriated and sold me to the slave dealer."

"What a shame and injustice!" Hadan Gula protested, "But tell me, how did you regain your freedom?"

"We shall come to that, but not yet. Let us continue my tale," said Sharru. "As we passed by the fields, the plowers jeered at us. One took off his ragged hat, bowed low, and called out, 'Welcome to Babylon, guests of the king! He waits for you on the city walls where the banquet awaits—mud bricks and onion soup!' With that they roared in laughter.

"Pirate flew into a rage and cursed them. I asked him, 'What do those men mean when they say the king awaits us on the walls?'

"'They will force you to march to the city walls to carry bricks until your back breaks!' roared Pirate. 'Or perhaps they will beat you to death before your back breaks. They won't beat me! I will kill them first!'

"Then Megiddo spoke up, and said, 'It makes little sense to speak of masters beating hardworking slaves to death. Masters like hardworking slaves and treat them well.'

"Then Zabado joined in. 'Who wants to work hard?' he commented. 'Those plowers are wise. They're not breaking their backs, they're just acting as though they are.'

"'You can't get ahead by pretending to do good work,' Megiddo protested. 'If you plow two or three acres, that's a good day's work, and any master knows it. But if you plow only half an acre, it doesn't matter how much you act as though you were working hard. I like to work and I like to do good work, for work is the best friend I've ever known. It has brought me the good things I've had—my farm, my cows and crops, everything.'

"Zabado huffed in contempt. He said to Megiddo, 'Well then, where are these things now? I figure it pays better to be smart and get by without working. You watch me, if they sell us to the walls. I'll be carrying a water bag or some easy job while you, who like to work, will break your back carrying bricks.' He laughed and laughed.

"Terror gripped me that night. I could not sleep. I lay down close to the guard rope, and when the others were asleep I attracted the attention of the guard, Godoso. He was a war-toughened, pillaging Arab, a rough man. If he robbed you, he would cut your throat as well.

"'Tell me Godoso,' I whispered, 'when we get to Babylon, will they sell us to the walls?'

"'Why you want to know?' he asked cautiously.

"'Can you not understand my plight?' I pleaded. 'I am young. I want to live. I don't want to be worked or beaten to death on the walls. Is there any chance for me to get a good master?'

"He whispered back, 'I tell you something. You good fellow, give Godoso no trouble. Most times we go first to slave market. When buyers come, tell 'em you good worker, like to work hard for good master. Make 'em want to buy. If you not make 'em buy, next day you carry brick. Mighty hard work.'

"After he walked away, I lay in the warm sand, looking up at the stars and thinking about work. What Megiddo had said about work being his best friend made me wonder if it might also be my best friend. Certainly it would be if it helped me out of this.

"When Megiddo awoke, I whispered the good news to him. It was our ray of hope as we marched to Babylon.

"We approached the walls late in the afternoon. What a sight! Lines of men, like black ants, climbing up and down the steep diagonal paths. As we drew closer, we were amazed at the thousands of men working. Some were digging the moat, others mixed the dirt into mud bricks. Most were carrying the bricks in large baskets up those steep trails to the masons.

"Overseers cursed those who didn't work hard, and cracked whips on the backs of those who didn't keep up. Poor, worn-out fellows staggered and fell beneath the heavy baskets of bricks, unable to rise again. If the lash failed to bring them to their feet, they were pushed to the side of the paths and left writhing in agony. Soon their bodies would be dragged down to join others beside the roadway to await their final resting place in a mass grave. As I beheld the ghastly sight, I shuddered. So this was what awaited my father's son if he failed at the slave market.

"Godoso had been right. They took us through the gates of the city to the slave prison, and the next morning marched us to the pens in the market. There the rest of the men huddled in fear, and only the whips of the guards could keep them moving them so the buyers could look them over. Megiddo and I eagerly talked to every man who permitted us to address him.

"Soldiers from the brutal king's guard purchased Pirate from the group and shackled him. When he protested, they beat him brutally and carried him away. I felt sorry for him.

"Megiddo knew we would soon part ways. When no buyers were around, he impressed upon me just how valuable work would be for me in the future. 'Some men hate it,' he said. 'They make it their enemy. It is much better to like it and make it your friend. Never mind that it is hard. If you build a fine house, who cares if the beams are heavy, or that it is far from the well to carry the water for the plaster? Promise me, boy, that if you get a master, you will work for him as hard as you can. If he does not appreciate how hard you work, pay it no mind. Remember, work well done is good for the man who does it. It makes him a better man.' He stopped talking as a burly farmer walked up to the enclosure and looked at us critically.

"Megiddo asked about his farm and crops and soon convinced him Megiddo would be a valuable man. After aggressive bargaining with the slave trader, the farmer pulled a fat purse from beneath his robe and soon Megiddo followed his new master out of sight.

"A few other men were sold during the morning. At noon, Godoso confided to me that the dealer was disgusted with the prices the buyers were willing to pay, and would not stay over another night. At sundown he would take all who remained to the king's buyer. I was becoming desperate, when a fat, good-natured man walked up and asked if there was a baker among us.

"I approached him and asked, 'Why would a great baker like yourself want an inferior baker? Wouldn't it be better to teach a willing man like myself how to do it the right way? I am young and strong, and I like to work. Give me a chance and I will do my best to earn gold and silver for your purse.'

"My willingness impressed him, and he began to bargain with the dealer who had not once noticed me since he bought me, but was now speaking grandly about my abilities, my good health, and good disposition. I felt like a fat ox being sold to the butcher. At last, to my great joy, the deal was closed. I followed my new master away, thinking I was the luckiest man in Babylon.

"My new home was much to my liking. Nana-naid, my master, taught me how to grind barley in the stone bowl in the courtyard, how to build the fire in the oven, and how to grind very fine sesame flour for honey cakes. I had a couch in the shed where the grain was stored. The old slave housekeeper, Swasti, fed me well and was pleased with the way I helped her with heavy tasks.

"Here was the chance I had longed for, to make myself valuable to my master and, I hoped, to find a way to earn my freedom.

"I asked Nana-naid to show me how to knead bread and to bake. He did, and my willingness to learn pleased him. When I had mastered these skills, I asked him to show me how to bake honey cakes. Soon I was doing all the baking. My master was glad to be free of the work, but Swasti shook her head in disapproval. 'To do no work is a bad thing for any man,' she declared.

"I felt it was time for me to think of a way to earn coins to buy my freedom. Since the baking was finished around noon every day, I thought Nana-naid would approve if I found profitable employment in the afternoons. I hoped he might even allow me to keep a share of the earnings. The thought came to me, why not bake more of the honey cakes and sell them to hungry men in the city streets?

"I presented my plan to Nana-naid this way: 'If I can use my afternoons after the baking is finished to earn coins for you, would it be fair for you to share the profits with me so I might have money of my own to spend?'

"'Fair enough, fair enough,' he admitted. When I told him of my plan to sell honey cakes, he was well pleased. 'Here is what we will do,' he suggested. 'You sell them at two for a shekel, then half of the shekels will be mine to pay for the flour, the honey, and the wood to bake them. Of the rest, I shall take half and you shall keep half.'

"I was very pleased with his generous offer that I might keep, for myself, one-fourth of my sales. That night, I worked late to make a tray on which to display the cakes. Nana-naid gave me one of his worn robes, so I might look presentable, and Swasti helped me patch it and wash it clean.

"The next day I baked an extra supply of honey cakes. They looked brown and tempting on the tray as I went down the street announcing my goods for sale. At first no one seemed interested, and I became discouraged. But I kept on. Late in the afternoon as men became hungry, the cakes began to sell. Word traveled quickly, and soon my tray was empty.

"Nana-naid was very pleased with my success and gladly paid me my share. I was delighted to hold shekels. Megiddo had been right when he said a master appreciated good work from his slaves. That night I was so excited about my success, I could hardly sleep. I lay awake calculating how much I could make in a moon, how much I could make in a year, and how many years it would take to buy my freedom.

"As I went forth with my tray of cakes every day, I soon found regular customers. One of these was your grandfather, Arad Gula. He was a rug merchant who sold to housewives, going from one end of the city to the other, accompanied by a mule loaded high with rugs, and a slave to assist him. Arad would buy two cakes for himself and two for his slave, and always lingered to talk with me while they ate them.

"Your grandfather said something to me I shall always remember. He said, 'I like your cakes, young man. But I like the enterprising spirit with which you offer them even more. Such spirit can carry you far on the road to success.'

"Can you possibly understand, Hadan Gula, what those words of encouragement could mean to me, a slave boy, alone in a great city, struggling with everything he had in him to find a way out of his humiliation?

"As the months rolled by I continued to add shekels to my purse. It began to have a comforting weight on my belt. Work was proving to be my best friend, just as Megiddo had said it would.

"But Swasti was worried.

"'Your master is spending too much time at the gambling houses,' she protested.

"Not long after, I was overjoyed one afternoon to see my friend Megiddo on the street. He was leading three mules loaded with vegetable for the market. 'I am doing mighty well,' he said. 'My master appreciates my good work, and now I am a foreman. He trusts me to bring his goods to the market, and he is sending for my family. Work is helping me recover from my great trouble. Someday it will help me buy my freedom so I may once again own a farm of my own.'

"Often, I went outside the city gates to solicit the overseers of the slaves building the walls. I hated the sight of those slaves and the brutality they were forced to endure, but the overseers were good buyers. One day I was surprised to see Zabado waiting in line to fill his basket with bricks. His body was gaunt and bent, and his back had welts and gashes from the whips of the overseers. I felt sorry for him, and handed him a cake, which he crammed into his mouth like a hungry animal. Seeing the greedy look in his eyes, I ran before he could grab my tray.

"'Why do you work so hard?' your grandfather asked me one day. It is the same question you asked me today, do you remember? I told him what Megiddo had said about work, and how it was proving to be my best friend. I showed him with pride my purse full of shekels, and explained that I was saving to buy my freedom.

"'What will you do when you are free?' he inquired.

"'I intend to become a merchant,' I answered.

"With that, he confided to me something I had never suspected. 'You don't know this, but I, too, am a slave. I am in partnership with my master.'"

"Stop!" demanded Hadan Gula. "I will not let you dishonor my grandfather Arad Gula! He was no slave!" His eyes blazed in anger.

Sharru Nada remained calm. "I honor him for rising above his misfortune and becoming a leading citizen of Damascus. You are his grandson. Are you not cut from the same cloth? Are you man enough to face the truth, or do you prefer to live under an illusion?"

Hadan sat up straight in his saddle. In a voice trembling with emotion he replied, "My grandfather was beloved by all. His good deeds were many. When the great famine came, did he not buy grain in Egypt, and with his caravan bring it to Damascus to feed the people so none would starve? Now you say he was a despised slave in Babylon?"

"Had he remained a slave in Babylon and thought himself so, he might indeed have been despised. But when, through his significant efforts, he became a great man of Damascus, the gods indeed overlooked his misfortunes and honored him with their respect," Sharru Nada replied.

"After telling me he was a slave," Sharru continued, "he explained how anxious he had been to earn his freedom. Now that he had enough money, he was troubled as to what he should do. He was no longer making good sales, and he feared leaving the support of his master.

"I protested his indecision. 'Cling no longer to your master. Regain for yourself the feeling of being a free man. Act like a free man and succeed like one! Decide what you want to accomplish, and then work will help you to achieve it!' As he went on his way he thanked me for my words, and said he was glad I had shamed him for his cowardice.

"One day I went outside of the gates again and was surprised to see an enormous crowd gathering there. When I asked a man for an explanation, he said, 'Have you not heard? An escaped slave, who murdered one of the king's guards, has been brought to justice and will this day be flogged to death for his crime. Even the king himself will be here.'

"The crowd was so dense around the flogging post, I dared not go near for fear they would upset my tray of honey cakes. Instead, I climbed to the top of the unfinished wall. From there I could see over the heads of the people. I was fortunate to see King Nebuchadnezzar himself as he rode by in his golden chariot. I had never beheld such grandeur, such magnificent robes sewn of gold cloth and velvet.

"I could not see the flogging of the slave, but I could hear the poor man as he shrieked in pain. I wondered how one as noble as our handsome king could endure such suffering. But when I saw that he was laughing and joking with the other royals, I knew he was cruel, and understood why the slaves building the walls were treated with such inhumanity.

"After the slave was dead, they hung his body on a pole by a rope tied to his leg, for all to see. As the crowd began to thin, I climbed down from the wall and went closer. I saw two entwined serpents tattooed on the slave's chest. It was Pirate.

"The next time I met Arad Gula he was a changed man. Full of enthusiasm, he greeted me. 'Behold, the slave you knew is now a free man!' he exclaimed. 'There was magic in your words. Already my sales and profits have increased. My wife desires that we move to a faraway city where no man shall know I was a slave, so our children will not have to suffer the shame. Work has become my best helper. It has enabled me to regain my confidence and my skills as a merchant.'

"I was overjoyed that I had been able, even in a small way, to repay him for the encouragement he had given me.

"One evening Swasti came to me in deep distress. 'Your master is in trouble,' she said. 'I fear for him. Some months ago he lost much gold at the gaming tables. He does not pay the farmer for his grain nor his honey. He does not pay the money lender. They are angry, and they threaten him.'

"'Why should we worry about his foolishness? We are not his keepers.' I replied thoughtlessly.

"'Foolish young man, you do not understand. He gave the money lender your title as collateral for a loan. Under the law, he can claim you and sell you. I do not know what to do. He is a good master. Why did trouble find him?'

"Swasti's fears were not unwarranted. The next morning when I was baking, the moneylender came with a man called Sasi. The man looked me over and said that I would do.

"The moneylender did not wait for my master, but told Swasti to tell him he had taken me. With only the robe on my back and my purse of shekels hanging safely from my belt, I was hurried away from my unfinished baking.

"They whirled me away from my dearest hopes as the cyclone snatches the tree from the forest and casts it into the surging sea. Once again, a gaming house and barley beer had caused me disaster.

"Sasi was a blunt, gruff man. As he led me across the city, I told him about the good work I had been doing for Nana-naid, and said I hoped to do good work for him as well. His reply offered no encouragement.

"He told me, 'The king has told my master to send me to build a section of the city's Grand Canal. I do not like that kind of work, nor does my master. He tells me to buy more slaves who will work hard and finish the task quickly. But how can any man finish such a big job so fast?'

"Picture a desert with not a tree, just low shrubs and a sun burning with such fury the water in our barrels became so hot we could scarcely drink it. Then picture rows of men, going down into the deep excavation and lugging heavy baskets of dirt up soft, dusty trails, then back down and up again from daylight until dark. Picture food served in troughs from which we helped ourselves like swine. We had no tents, no straw for beds. That was the situation in which I found myself. I buried my purse in a marked spot, wondering if I would ever dig it up again.

"At first I worked with good will, but as the months dragged on I felt my spirit breaking. Then the heat fever took hold of my weary body. I lost my appetite and could scarcely eat the mutton and vegetables. At night I would toss in unhappy sleeplessness.

"In my misery, I wondered if Zabbado had been right to only pretend to work hard rather than break his back under a heavy load. Then I recalled my last sight of him and knew his plan was a bad one.

"I thought of Pirate with his bitterness, and wondered if it might be just as well to fight and kill. Then I recalled his bleeding body and his screams, and knew his plan could only lead to tragedy.

"Then I remembered the last time I had seen Megiddo. His hands were deeply callused from hard work, but his heart was light and there was happiness in his face. His was the best plan.

"Yet I was just as willing to work as Megiddo; he could not have worked harder than I. Why did my work not bring me happiness and success? Was it work that brought Megiddo happiness, or was happiness and success merely in the hands of the gods? Was I to work the rest of my life without realizing my desires, without happiness or success? All of these questions were jumbled in my mind, but I had no answer. Indeed, I was sorely confused.

"Several days later, when it seemed I had reached the end of my endurance and my questions remained unanswered, Sasi sent for me. A messenger had come with word that I had a new master, who demanded I be brought back to Babylon. I dug up my precious purse, wrapped myself in the remnants of my robe, and was on my way.

"As we rode, the same thoughts of a cyclone whirling me hither and thither kept racing through my feverish brain. I seemed to be living the words of an old chant from my native town of Harroun:

Besetting a man like a whirlwind,
Driving him like a storm,
Whose course no one can follow,
Whose destiny no one can foretell.

"Was I destined to be punished forever, for reasons I could not fathom? What new miseries and disappointments awaited me?

"When we rode to the courtyard of my new master's house, imagine my surprise when I saw Arad Gula awaiting me. He helped me down from the horse and hugged me like a long-lost brother.

"As we went on our way, I tried to follow him as a slave should follow his master, but he would not permit me. He put his arm around me, saying, 'I hunted everywhere for you. When I had almost given up hope, I met Swasti, who told me about the moneylender, who directed me to your noble owner. He drove a hard bargain, and made me pay an outrageous price. But you are worth it. Your philosophy and your enterprising spirit have been the inspiration for my success.'

"'It was Megiddo's philosophy,' I told him, 'not mine.'

"'Megiddo's and yours, then. Thanks to you both. We are going to Damascus, and I need you to be my partner.' With that, he threw back his robe and held a clay tablet carrying my title. 'See,' he exclaimed, 'in a moment you will be a free man!' He raised the tablet above his head and hurled it to the ground, breaking it into a hundred pieces on the cobblestones. Gleefully he stomped on the fragments until they were nothing more than dust.

"Tears of gratitude filled my eyes. I knew I was the luckiest man in Babylon.

"Surely you see by this, Hadan Gula, that work, in the time of my greatest distress, proved to be my best friend. My willingness to work enabled me to escape from being sold to join the slave gangs upon the walls. It also impressed your grandfather so much that he selected me to be his partner."

Then Hadan Gula asked, "Was work also my grandfather's secret key to acquiring gold?"

"It was the only key he had when I first knew him," Sharru replied. "Your grandfather enjoyed working. The gods appreciated his efforts and rewarded him generously."

"I am starting to see." Hadan was speaking thoughtfully. "Work attracted his many friends who admired his industry and the success it brought. Work brought him the honors he enjoyed in Damascus.

Work brought him all those things I have admired. And I thought work was fit only for slaves."

"Life is rich with many pleasures for men to enjoy," Sharru Nada commented. "Each has its place. I am glad that work is not reserved for slaves. If that were the case I would be deprived of my greatest pleasure. There are many things I enjoy, but nothing takes the place of work."

Sharru Nada and Hadan Gula rode in the shadows of the towering walls up to the massive bronze gates of Babylon. As they approached, the gate guards jumped to attention and respectfully saluted an honored citizen. Sharru held his head high as he led the long caravan through the gates and up the streets of the city.

"I have always hoped to be a man like my grandfather," Hadan confided to him. "I never before realized just what kind of man he was. You have shown me. Now that I understand, I admire him all the more, and feel more determined to be like him. I fear I can never repay you for giving me the true key to his success. From this day forward I shall use his key. I shall start humbly, as he started, which befits my true station far better than jewels and fine robes."

With those words, Hadan Gula pulled the jeweled baubles from his ears and the rings from his fingers. He then reined in his horse, dropped back, and rode with deep respect behind the leader of the caravan.

CHAPTER FIVE

The Goddess of Good Luck

Among the towered buildings in Babylon was one that ranked in importance with the Palace of the King, the Hanging Gardens, and the temples of the gods. It exerted a powerful influence on the thought of that time. This building was the Temple of Learning, a gathering place for those who sought wisdom. The temple had walls and walls of shelved clay tablets, organized by subject—math, finance, architecture, art, canal engineering, and so forth. There were also many classrooms where wisdom of the past was expounded on by voluntary teachers, and where subjects of popular interest were discussed in open forums. Within the walls, all men were equal. The humblest of slaves was free to debate and dispute the opinions of a prince of the royal house.

Among the many who frequented the temple of learning was a wise, rich man named Arkad, called the richest man in Babylon. He had his own special hall, where almost any evening a large group of men, some old, some very young, but mostly middle-aged, gathered to discuss and argue interesting subjects.

The sun had just set like a great red ball of fire shining through the haze of desert dust when Arkad strolled to his accustomed platform. Already, more than eighty men were awaiting his arrival, reclining on their small rugs spread upon the floor. More were still arriving.

"What shall we discuss tonight?" Arkad inquired.

After a brief hesitation, a tall cloth weaver addressed him, rising from his rug, as was the custom. "I have a subject I would like to hear discussed. I hesitate to offer it, though, as it may seem ridiculous to you, Arkad, and to my good friends here." When urged to offer it, by Arkad as well as the others, he continued. "Today I have been lucky, for I have found a purse filled with pieces of gold. It is my great desire to continue to be lucky, and I feel that all men share that desire. I suggest we debate how to attract good luck, so we may discover ways it can be enticed to become a loyal companion."

"A most interesting subject has been offered," Arkad commented, "one most worthy of our discussion. To some men, luck is just a chance event that, like an accident, may happen to a man without cause or reason. Others believe that the instigator of all good luck is Ashtar, our most bounteous Goddess of Good Luck, who is always eager to reward those who please her, and will bless them with generous gifts. Speak up, my friends. What do you say? Shall we seek to discover whether good luck can be enticed to visit each and every one of us?

"Yes! Yes! And much of it!" responded the growing group of eager listeners.

With that, Arkad continued, "To start our discussion, let us first hear from those among us who have enjoyed experiences similar to that of the cloth weaver in finding or receiving, with no effort on their part, valuable treasures or jewels."

There was a pause, each man expecting another to reply. No one did.

"What, no one speaks?" Arkad said. "Then this kind of luck must be rare indeed. Let us then discuss the matter in a different way. Who among you has had good luck within reach, only to see it escape?" Arkad asked.

This time many hands were raised, among them that of an elderly merchant.

"Speak up, sir," said Arkad. "Kindly share your story."

The merchant stood up to speak, smoothing his elegant white robe. "With your permission, most honorable Arkad and friends, I will gladly share a tale that illustrates how close good luck may approach a man and how blindly he may allow it to escape, much to his loss and later regret.

"Many years ago, when I was a young man, just married and already earning a decent income, my father came to me and strongly urged me to invest in a project. The son of his good friend had found a barren piece of land just outside the outer walls of our city. It lay high above the canal, where no water could reach it.

"The son of my father's friend had devised a plan to purchase this land, and build three water wheels that could be operated by oxen to bring water to the fertile soil. Once this was accomplished, he planned to divide the land into small tracts, which he would sell to residents of the city for growing crops.

"The son of my father's friend did not possess sufficient gold to complete such an undertaking. Like myself, he was a young man just beginning to earn a fair sum of money. His father, like mine, was a man of a large family and small means. For that reason he decided to enlist a group of men to join him in the enterprise. He would select twelve investors, each of whom would agree to pay one-tenth of his earnings into the project until the land was made ready for sale. Each man would then receive a fair share of the profits in proportion to his investment.

"My father spoke earnestly to me of this opportunity. 'You, my son, are young,' he said. 'It is my deep desire that you begin now to build a valuable estate for yourself, so you may become wealthy and respected among men. I wish to see you profit from an understanding of the thoughtless mistakes of your father.'

"'I want this also, my father,' I replied.

"'Then, this is what I advise,' said my father. 'Do what I should have done at your age. From your earnings, reserve one-tenth to put into favorable investments. With this one-tenth of your earnings and also what your investments will earn, you can accumulate for yourself a valuable estate long before you reach the age I am now.'

"'Your words are wise, Father,' I responded. 'I desire riches. But there are many things drawing me to spend the earnings I have, so I hesitate to do as you advise. I am young. There is plenty of time to think about building my fortune.'

"'I thought so, too, at your age,' my father replied. 'And yet, as you see, many years have passed and still I have not begun.'

"'We live in a different age, Father. I shall avoid your mistakes.'

"'Opportunity stands before you, my son. It is offering a chance that may lead to wealth. I beg of you, do not delay. Go tomorrow to the son of my friend and bargain with him to allow you to pay one-tenth of your earnings into this investment. Go promptly at sunrise. Opportunity waits for no man. Today it is here; soon it is gone. Therefore, do not delay!'

The merchant continued, "Despite my father's advice, I did hesitate. There were beautiful new robes just brought by the tradesmen from the east, robes of such richness and beauty that my wife and I felt each of us must possess one. If I agreed to invest one-tenth of my earnings in the enterprise as my father advised, then we must deprive ourselves of these and other pleasures we dearly wanted. I delayed making my decision until it was too late, much to my later regret. The enterprise proved to be far more profitable than any man had expected. This is my tale, which shows how I allowed good luck to escape."

A rugged-looking man from the desert rose from his blanket and spoke. "In this tale we see how good luck comes only to the man who welcomes opportunity when it arrives at his door. The building of an estate requires a beginning. That beginning may be just a few pieces of silver or gold that a man sets aside from his earnings to make his first investment. I now have great wealth as the owner of many herds. I began when I was just a boy, and purchased a young calf with a single piece of silver. That first small purchase was of great importance to me, as it marked the beginning of building my wealth.

"Taking the first step to building an estate is the best luck that can come to any man. That first step is of great importance, for it changes a man from one who earns money from his own labor to one who draws earnings by investing his gold. Some, fortunately, take it when they are young, and accumulate much more than those who start later in life, or who, even worse, like the father of this merchant, never start at all.

"If our friend the merchant had taken this first step in his early manhood, when this opportunity presented itself, today he would be blessed with more of this world's goods. At least he has learned from his mistake. Now if our friend the cloth weaver takes his good luck in finding a purse filled with gold, and uses it wisely, it will indeed be the beginning of much greater good fortune."

A stranger from another country arose. "Thank you!" he exclaimed. "I also like to speak. I am Syrian. I have much trouble to speak your language. I wish to call this friend, the merchant, a name. Maybe you think it is not polite, this name. But still, I wish to call him this. Alas, I do not know your word for it. So please, some good gentleman, tell me that right name you call man who puts off doing those things that be good for him."

"Procrastinator," called a voice.

"That's it!" shouted the Syrian, waving his hands excitedly. "He does not welcome opportunity when she comes. He waits. He says, 'I am busy now. One day I talk to you.' Opportunity, though, she will not wait for such slow fellow. She thinks if a man desires to be lucky he will step quick. Any man who does not step quick when opportunity comes, he big procrastinator like our friend, this merchant."

The other listeners laughed, and the merchant arose and bowed good naturedly in response. "My admiration to you, stranger within our gates, who does not hesitate to speak the truth."

"And now, let us hear another tale of opportunity. Who has another experience to share with us?" demanded Arkad.

"I do," responded a middle-aged man in a fine red robe. "I am a buyer of animals, mostly horses and camels, sometimes sheep and goats. The tale I am about to share is the true story of how opportunity came to me one night when I least expected it. Perhaps that is the reason I let it escape. You shall be the judge.

"I returned one evening to the city after a disheartening ten-day journey in search of camels to buy, and was angered to find the gates of the city closed and locked. While my slaves spread our tent for the night, which we prepared to pass with little food and no water, I was approached by an elderly farmer who, like us, found himself locked outside the city.

"'Kind sir,' he addressed me, 'from your appearance, I presume you are a buyer. If this is true, I would like very much to sell you this excellent flock of sheep I have just driven up. Alas, my good wife lies very sick with the fever. I must return with all haste to be by her side. Please buy my sheep so that I and my slaves may mount our camels and travel back to her without delay.'

"It was so dark that I could not see his flock, but I could tell it was a large flock by the sound of their bleating. Having wasted ten days searching for camels I could not find, I was glad to bargain with him. In his anxiety, he set a most reasonable price. I accepted, knowing my slaves could drive the flock through the city gates in the morning and sell at a substantial profit.

"Once we agreed upon the price, I called my slaves to bring torches so we could count the flock, which the farmer declared numbered nine hundred sheep. I shall not burden you, my friends, with a description of our difficulty in attempting to count so many thirsty, restless, and milling sheep. It was an impossible task. Therefore, I bluntly informed the farmer I would count them at daylight and pay him then.

"'Please, good sir,' he pleaded. 'Pay me just two-thirds of the price tonight, so I may be on my way. I will leave my most intelligent and educated slave to assist you in counting in the morning. He is trustworthy, and you can pay him the balance.'

"But I was stubborn, wanted to be certain, and refused to make payment that night. The next morning, before I awoke, the city gates opened and four buyers rushed out in search of flocks. They were eager to pay high prices because Babylon's enemies had threatened the city with a siege, and the city needed a good supply of food. The old farmer received nearly three times the price he had offered me for the flock. In this way I allowed exceptional good luck to escape."

"It is an unusual tale," commented Arkad. "What wisdom does it suggest?"

"The wisdom of making payment immediately when we are convinced a good bargain is at hand," suggested an esteemed saddle maker. "If the bargain is good, that is when you need protection against your own weaknesses as much as you need protection against any other man. We mortals are changeable. Alas, I must say we are more apt to change our minds when we are right than when we are wrong. When wrong, we are stubborn indeed. When right, we are inclined to vacillate and let opportunity escape. My first judgment is my best. Yet I have always found it difficult to compel myself to proceed with a good bargain once I've made it. Therefore, as a protection against my own weaknesses, I make a prompt deposit on it. This saves me from later regrets for losing the good luck that should have been mine."

The Syrian was on his feet once more. "Thank you! Again, I like to speak. These tales much alike. Each time, opportunity fly away for same reason. Each time she come to procrastinator, bringing good plan. Each time they hesitate, not say, 'Right now best time, I do it quick.' How can men succeed this way?"

"Your words are wise, my friend," responded the buyer of animals. "Good luck fled in both these tales because of procrastination. But this is not unusual. The spirit of procrastination is within all men. We desire riches, yet often when opportunity appears we hesitate to accept it. In listening to that urge to procrastinate, we become our own worst enemies.

"In my younger days, I did not know the word procrastination. I thought at first it was my own poor judgement that caused me to lose many profitable trades. Later, I attributed it to my stubborn disposition, or because I wanted certainty. At last, I recognized it for what it was—a habit of delaying when prompt and decisive action was required. I hated it when I realized this was the cause of my misfortune. With the bitterness of a wild mule hitched to a chariot, I broke loose from this enemy of my success."

"Thank you! I like ask question to Mr. Merchant," the Syrian continued. "You wear fine robes, not like those of poor man. You speak like successful man. Tell us, do you still listen when procrastination whisper in your ear?"

"Like our friend the buyer, I also had to recognize it and conquer procrastination," responded the merchant. "To me, it proved to be an enemy, ever watching and waiting, ready to pounce and thwart my accomplishments. The tale I related is just one of many I could tell of how it drove away my opportunities.

"Once understood, it is not difficult to conquer. No man willingly permits the thief to rob his bins of grain. Nor does any man willingly permit an enemy to drive away his customers and rob him of his profits. Once I recognized that this enemy, procrastination, was committing these very acts, I vowed to conquer it. So must every man master his own spirit of procrastination before he can expect to share in the rich treasures of Babylon.

"What do you say, Arkad?" the merchant went on. "You are the richest man in Babylon, and that is why many say you are the luckiest. Do you agree with me that no man can succeed to the fullest until he has completely crushed the spirit of procrastination within him?"

"Yes, it is as you say," Arkad admitted. "During my long life I have watched generation after generation, marching forward in the areas of trade, science, and learning that lead to success in life. Opportunities came to all these men. Some grasped theirs and moved steadily toward the gratification of their deepest desires, but the majority hesitated, faltered, and fell behind."

Arkad turned to the cloth weaver. "It was you who suggested that we debate good luck. Tell us, what do you think about it now?"

"I see good luck in a different light. I had thought of it as something very desirable that might happen to a man with no effort on his part. Now I realize that to attract good luck, one must take advantage of opportunities. Therefore, in the future I will endeavor to make the best of each opportunity that comes my way."

"You have grasped the simple truths brought forth in our discussion," Arkad replied. "Good luck, we find, often follows opportunity, but seldom comes otherwise. Our merchant friend would have found great good luck if he had acted on the investment opportunity the Goddess of Good Luck presented him, as his father advised. Our friend the buyer, likewise, would have enjoyed good luck had he completed the purchase of the flock of sheep, and sold for a handsome profit.

"We pursued this discussion to find a way to entice good luck to enter our lives. I feel we have found a way. Both the merchant's tale and that of the buyer illustrate how good luck follows opportunity—

but only if one is willing to act on it. Many find reasons to wait, but often procrastination allows good luck to turn her attention to another man. Here lies a truth that many similar tales of good luck, won or lost, cannot change: A man can attract good luck by accepting opportunity and acting on it.

"Those who are eager to grasp opportunities to improve their lives do attract the attention of the Goddess of Good Luck. She is eager to help those who please her. Men who take decisive action please her best. Therefore, if a plan is in your best interest, promptly accept it. If it is against your best interest, with equal promptness reject it.

"Action will lead you forward to the success you desire."

The Goddess of Good Luck
favors men of action.

CHAPTER SIX

The Gold Lender of Babylon

Fifty pieces of gold! Never had Rodan, the spear maker of old Babylon, had so much gold in his purse. He strode happily down the king's highway from the palace of his most generous Majesty with his head high. The gold clinked cheerfully as the purse at his belt swayed with every step he took—the sweetest music he had ever heard.

Fifty pieces of gold! All his! Rodan could hardly believe his great fortune. What power in those clinking coins! They could purchase anything he wanted—a grand house, land, cattle, camels, horses, chariots, whatever he might desire.

What should he do with it? On that day, as he turned into a side street toward the home of his sister, he could think of nothing he would rather possess than those glittering, heavy pieces of gold—all his to keep.

It was on an evening a few days later that a perplexed Rodan entered the shop of Mathon, the gold lender and dealer in jewels and rare fabrics. He passed through the shop, ignoring the many colorful wares artfully displayed, and headed straight to the living quarters at the back. There he found the distinguished Mathon lounging on a rug, enjoying a fine meal served by a slave.

"I need your advice," Rodan said, "for I know not what to do." He stood upright, with dignity.

Mathon's thin, pale face smiled a friendly greeting. "What indiscretions have you committed that you should seek the help of a lender of gold? Have you been unlucky at the gaming table? Or become entangled in the charms of a woman? I have known you for many years, yet never before have you asked for my help."

"No, no. Nothing like that. I am not seeking gold. Instead I need your wise advice."

"What? Do my ears deceive me? No one comes to the lender of gold for advice."

"Indeed, you heard correctly."

"Can this be so? Rodan, the spear maker, is more clever than all the rest, because he comes to Mathon not for gold, but for advice. Men come to me for gold to pay for their follies, but never for advice. Yet who is better able to give advice than the lender of gold, to whom many men come when they are in trouble?

"You shall eat with me, Rodan," he continued. "You shall be my guest for the evening. Andol!" he called to his slave. "Draw up a rug for my friend, Rodan, the spear maker, who has come for advice. He shall be my honored guest. Bring him great platters of food and get him my largest cup, then choose from my best wine so he may enjoy our feast."

Mathon turned to his friend. "Now, tell me what troubles you."

"It is the king's gift."

"The king's gift? The king gave you a gift and it troubles you? What kind of gift?"

"Because he was so pleased with the design I submitted to him for a new point on the spears of the royal guard, he presented me with fifty pieces of gold. Now I am severely perplexed."

Rodan continued, "Every hour of the day I am approached by someone who asks that I share it with him."

"That is natural," Mathon said with a nod. "There are far more men who want gold than there are men who have it, and many believe those who have it should be willing to share it. But can you not say 'No'? Is your will not as strong as your fist?"

"To most I can say no, but sometimes it would be easier to say yes. Can one refuse to share with one's sister, to whom he is deeply devoted?"

"Surely your own sister would not wish to deprive you of enjoying your reward."

"No, Mathon. But she asks for the sake of Araman, her husband. She hopes to see him become a rich merchant, but feels he has never had a chance. She believes that if I loan him this gold, he will become prosperous and repay me from his profits."

"My friend," resumed Mathon, "it is a worthy subject you bring to discuss with me. He who acquires gold acquires responsibility along with it, and a changed position in the eyes of his fellow men. Gold brings fear that he might make poor decisions and lose it, or have it swindled from him. It brings a feeling of power and the opportunity to do good. But it also brings the possibility that his best intentions might bring him difficulties.

"Did you hear about the farmer from Nineveh who could understand the language of animals? I expect you have not, for it is not a tale commonly shared. I will tell you the story, for you should know there is more to borrowing and lending than simply the passing of gold from one hand to another.

"This farmer, who could understand what animals say to each other, would sit in the barnyard each evening just to listen to them. One evening he heard the ox complaining to the mule about how difficult his job was. 'I must pull the plow from morning until night,' he moaned. 'No matter how hot the day or how tired my legs, or how much the harness chafes my neck, still I must pull. But you are a creature of leisure. You wear a colorful blanket and do nothing more than carry our master where he wants to go. When he goes nowhere, you rest and eat green grass all day. It is not just.'

"Now, the mule, in spite of his vicious heels, was a good fellow, and sympathized with the ox. 'My good friend,' he replied, 'you do work very hard, and I would like to help you. Therefore, I will tell you how you may have a day of rest. In the morning when the slave comes to fetch you, lie upon the ground and bellow loudly. He will say you are sick and cannot work.'

"So, the next morning the ox took the advice of the mule and, as was foretold, the slave returned to the farmer and told him the ox was sick and could not pull the plow.

"'Then,' said the farmer, 'hitch the mule to the plow, for the plowing must be done.'

"All day long the mule, who had only intended to help his friend, was compelled to perform the ox's task. When night came and he was at last released from the plow, his heart was bitter, his legs were weary, and his neck was sore where the harness had chafed it.

"That night the farmer lingered in the barnyard to listen.

"The ox began first. 'You are a good friend,' he said to the mule. 'Because of your wise advice I have enjoyed a day of rest.'

"'And I,' retorted the mule, 'am like many others who start out to help a friend and end up doing his task for him. From this point forward, you draw your own plow, for I heard the master tell the slave to send for the butcher if you were sick another day. I wish he would, for you are a lazy fellow.' After that, they never spoke to one another again.

"Can you tell me the moral of this story, Rodan?"

"It is a good tale," Rodan said, "but I do not see the moral."

"I did not think you would. But it is there, and it is a simple one. It is this: If you desire to help a friend, do it in a way that your friend's burdens do not become your own."

"I had not thought of that. It is a wise moral. I do not wish to carry the burdens of my sister's husband. But tell me. You lend to many people. Do borrowers not repay?"

Mathon smiled a smile made wise by experience. "Is it possible to make a good loan if the borrower cannot repay? Must not the lender be wise and judge carefully whether the borrower will use the gold wisely and return it to the lender, or whether it will be wasted and leave the borrower with a debt he cannot repay? I will show you debtors' tokens in my token chest, and let them tell you their stories."

Into the room Mathon brought a large, ornate chest covered in red pigskin and bronze. He put it on the floor and placed both hands on the lid. He closed his eyes and drew a heavy sigh.

"From each person to whom I lend gold, I demand a token for my token chest, to remain there until the debt is repaid. When they repay, I give it back. But if they don't, the token remains with me, forever reminding me of one who was not worthy of my confidence.

"The safest loans, my token box tells me, are to those whose possessions have more value than the loan they desire. They own land, jewels, camels, or other things they could sell to pay the loan. Some of the tokens given to me are jewels more valuable than the loan. Others are promises that if they do not repay, I will receive a piece of property. On loans like these, I know my gold can be returned along with the interest due, because the loan is based on property.

"In another class of borrowers are those who have the ability to earn. They are like you, who can work or serve and be paid. They have a steady income, and if they are honest and suffer no unforeseen hardship, I know they, too, can repay the gold I loan them as well as the interest to which I am entitled. These loans are based on human effort.

"Others have neither property nor earning power. Life is hard, and there will always be men who cannot adjust. My token box tells me that these loans, while small, may never be repaid unless they are guaranteed by a family member or friend of the borrower who knows him to be honorable."

Mathon released the clasp and opened the lid. Rodan leaned forward eagerly.

At the top of the chest, a bronze neck piece lay upon a scarlet cloth. Mathon picked up the neck piece and patted it affectionately. "This shall always remain in my token chest because the owner passed away. I treasure it, his token, and I treasure his memory, for he was my good friend. We traded together many years and did well, until he married a beautiful woman from a faraway land. He spent his gold lavishly on her to satisfy her endless desires. He came to me in distress when he had spent all his money. I counseled him. I told him I would help him to once more manage his own affairs. He swore he would do the things he needed to do. But it was not to be. In a quarrel, he dared his wife to put a knife in his heart, and she did."

"And she?" asked Rodan.

"Yes, of course, this was hers." Mathon picked up the scarlet cloth. "In bitter remorse, she threw herself into the Euphrates. These loans will never be repaid. What this chest tells you, Rodan, is that humans who are overwhelmed with emotions are not safe risks for the lender.

"Here! Now this one is different." He reached for a ring carved of ox bone. "This belongs to a farmer. I buy the rugs made by his wives to sell in my shop. The locusts came and ate his crops, so I helped him. When the new crop came, he repaid me. One day, he came to me and told me of unique goats in a distant land, as described by a traveler. They had long hair so fine and soft, it would weave into rugs more beautiful than any ever seen in Babylon. The farmer wanted a herd, but had no money. So I lent him some to make the journey and bring back goats. He gained a herd, and within a year I will surprise the lords of Babylon when I offer them the most beautiful and expensive rugs they have ever had the good fortune to buy. Soon it will be time to return this ring, as the farmer insists on repaying promptly."

"Some borrowers do that?" Rodan asked.

"If they borrow for the purpose of making money, it happens often. But if they borrow because of their indiscretions, I warn you to be cautious if you wish to have your gold back in hand again."

"So, tell me about this," Rodan requested, picking up a heavy gold bracelet inset with jewels in a rare design.

"You do like the ladies?" bantered Mathon.

"I am still much younger than you," retorted Rodan.

"I'll give you that. But this time you anticipate romance where there is none. The owner of this has not taken care of herself. She is wrinkled beyond her years and obese. She talks much and says little. It drives me mad. Once she had a lot of money and was a good customer, but she came upon hard times. She wanted her son to be a merchant. So she came to me and borrowed gold so he could become a partner of a caravan owner who travels with his camels, buying goods in one city and selling them in another.

"Unfortunately, his partner was a scoundrel. They traveled to a distant city and, while the boy slept, he took the money and left. Perhaps when the boy grows up he will repay. Until then I get no interest on the loan—only much talk. Fortunately, the jewels are worthy of the loan."

"Did the boy's mother ask for your advice about whether it was wise for her to take a loan?"

"Quite the opposite. In fact, she pictured her son as a wealthy and powerful man of Babylon. To suggest anything else was to infuriate her. I tried, and she rebuked me soundly. I knew the risks this inexperienced boy would face, but since she offered security, I could not refuse her.

"This," continued Mathon, waving a knotted rope, "belongs to Nebatur, the camel trader. When he wants to buy a herd larger than his funds, he brings me this knot and I lend him according to his needs. He is a wise trader. I have confidence in his good judgment and can lend to him freely. Many other merchants of Babylon have my confidence because of their honorable behavior and history. Good merchants are an asset to our community, and it benefits me to assist them in keeping trade moving so Babylon may be prosperous."

Mathon picked out a beetle carved in turquoise and tossed it on the floor in contempt. "A stone bug brought back from Egypt. The lad who owns it doesn't care if I ever get paid back. When I ask him about it, he replies, 'With my bad luck, how can I repay you? You don't need the money, you have plenty more.'

"What can I do? The token is his father's—a worthy man of modest means who pledged to me his land and herd to back his son's enterprises. The youth found success at first, and then became too greedy in his quest to gain great wealth. His knowledge was immature, and his businesses failed.

"Youth is ambitious. Youth tries to take short cuts to wealth and the desirable things that come with it. To acquire wealth quickly, the young often borrow unwisely. Lacking experience, they cannot understand that excessive debt is like a hopeless pit in which one may descend quickly, and where one may struggle in vain to get out. It is a pit of sorrow and regret.

"Do not misunderstand. I do not discourage borrowing. In the right situation, when it is done for a wise purpose, I recommend it. I myself became a successful merchant with borrowed gold.

"Yet, what is a lender to do in such a case? The youth is in despair and accomplishes nothing. Discouraged, he does not even try to repay. And yet, my heart prevents me from taking his father's land and cattle."

"You have told me much of what I wanted and needed to hear," said Rodan. "But I hear no answer to my question. Should I lend my fifty pieces of gold to my sister's husband? They both mean a great deal to me, and I want to help."

"Your sister is an honorable woman, and I think highly of her. If her husband came to me and asked to borrow fifty pieces of gold, I would ask him how he would he use it.

"If he answered he wanted to become a merchant like myself and deal in jewels and fine furnishings, I would then say, 'What knowledge do you have of this trade? Do you know where to buy at the lowest cost? Do you know where you can sell at a fair price?' Could Araman say 'Yes' to these questions?"

"No, he could not," Rodan admitted. "He has helped me quite a lot in making spears, and he has helped some in the shops."

"Then I would say to him that his purpose was not wise. Merchants must learn their trade. His ambition is worthy but not practical, and I would not lend him any gold.

"But suppose he said, 'Yes, I have helped merchants for many years. I know how to travel to Smyrna and to buy at low cost the rugs the housewives weave. I also know rich people in Babylon who would love the rugs and pay nicely.' Then I would say, 'Your purpose is wise and your ambition honorable. I will lend you the fifty gold pieces if you can give me security for the loan.' But if he then said, 'I have no security, but I am an honorable man and will pay you substantial interest on the loan.' Then I would reply, 'I treasure each piece of gold. If robbers were to take it from you as you were traveling to Smyrna, or take the rugs from you as you returned, you would have no means of repaying me and my gold would be gone.'

"Gold, my dear Rodan, is the merchandise of the money lender. It is easy to lend. But if it is lent unwisely, it is difficult to get back. The wise lender does not want the risk of the undertaking, but the guarantee of safe repayment.

"It is good," he continued, "to help those in trouble, those who are facing difficult times. It is also good to help those just starting out, so they may become productive citizens. But you must give help wisely, or else, like the farmer's mule, in your desire to help you may do little more than take on a burden that belongs to another.

"Again I strayed from your question, Rodan, but hear my answer: Keep your fifty pieces of gold. What your labor earns and what is given to you as a reward is yours, and no man can compel you to part with it unless it is your wish to do so. If you do want to lend it so that it may earn you more gold, then do so with much caution and in many places. I do not like to leave my gold sitting idle, but I like excessive risk even less.

"Tell me, my friend, how many years have you labored as a spear maker?"

"Three full years."

"How much, besides the king's gift, have you saved?"

"Three gold pieces."

"Each year that you have labored, you denied yourself things you desired, to save one piece of gold?"

"Yes."

"At that rate it would take you fifty years of labor and self-denial to accumulate fifty pieces of gold, yes?"

"That is true. It would be a lifetime of labor."

"Do you think your sister would wish to jeopardize the savings from fifty years of your labor just so her husband might experiment on being a merchant?"

"When I hear it in your words, no, I do not believe she would."

"Then go to her and say, 'For three years I have labored every day except fasting days, from morning until night. I have denied myself many things my heart craved, so that I might save as much as I could. For each year of labor and self-denial, I have one piece of gold to show for it. You are my dear sister, and I wish for your husband to become a merchant and prosper greatly. I long to help him as you have asked. If he will submit to me a plan that seems wise and probable to my friend, Mathon, I will gladly lend him my savings of an entire year so he may prove he can succeed.' Do that, and if he has the soul to succeed, he can prove it. If he fails, he will not owe you more than he can hope to someday repay.

"I am a gold lender because I own more gold than I can use in my own trade. I want to put my gold to work by lending it to others and thereby earn more gold. However, I do not want the risk of losing my gold, because I have worked hard and denied myself much to secure it. Therefore, I will no longer lend any of it unless I am confident it will be safe and promptly returned.

"I have shared with you, Rodan, a few of the secrets of my token chest. From those secrets, it is my hope that you will come to understand the weakness of men and their eagerness to borrow, even when they have no certain means to repay. They dream of great wealth and say, 'If only I had the gold to start, my earnings would surely be great.' But too often those dreams are nothing more than false hopes, because the men lack the ability or training to fulfill them.

"You now have more gold, Rodan, than you need, and you should put it to work for you. Soon you will become like me, a gold lender. If you employ it well, your gold will produce a rich source of pleasure and profit for the rest of your life. But if you let it escape, it will be a source of never-ending regret and sorrow, also for as long as you live.

"What do you want most from this gold you carry in your purse?"

"To keep it safe."

"Spoken wisely," replied Mathon with a nod of approval. "Safety is your first desire. Do you think it would be truly safe in the custody of your sister's husband?"

"I'm afraid not, for he is not wise in safeguarding gold."

"Then don't let foolish feelings of obligation sway you to trust anyone else with your treasure. If you want to help your family or your friends, find ways other than risking your wealth. Gold slips away in unexpected ways from those unskilled at guarding it. You would do better to waste it on your own extravagance than to give it to others to lose.

"What next, after safety, do you wish for this treasure of yours?"

"That it earn more gold,"

"Again, a wise answer. It should be put to work earning more gold. Gold wisely lent may even double itself before a man like you grows old. If you risk losing what you have, you risk losing all that it might earn, as well.

"And so, do not be swayed by the fantastic schemes of men who believe they can deliver extraordinary earnings in the blink of an eye. Such plans are the dreams of impractical men who are unskilled in the safe and dependable laws of wealth. Be conservative in what you expect your gold to earn, so that you may keep your treasure, grow it, and enjoy it. To hire it out on a promise of outlandish returns with little risk is to invite—and often to guarantee—loss.

"Seek to find established, successful, ethical merchants whom you may help. Your treasure will earn you generous profits under their skillful use, and their wisdom and experience will guard it safely. In this way you will avoid the mistakes many make when they have stewardship of gold."

When Rodan tried to thank Mathon for his sage advice, he would not listen. He said, "The king's gift will teach you many lessons. If you wish to keep your fifty pieces of gold, you must be discreet. Many uses will tempt you. Much advice will come your way. You will be offered many opportunities to make large profits. The stories from my token box should warn you, before you let a piece of gold leave your purse, be sure you have a safe way to pull it back. If you find my advice useful, come to see me again. I will gladly help you.

"Before you go, read the words I have carved beneath the lid of my token box. They apply equally to the borrower and the lender."

Better a little caution
than a great regret.

CHAPTER SEVEN

The Richest Man in Babylon

Arkad, the richest man in Babylon, had a system for becoming financially independent, one that offers a way for any man to have blessings beyond his dreams. In this chapter he shares his system without cost or obligation, as a gift to you. Will you accept it?

In old Babylon, Arkad was known far and wide for his great wealth. He was also well known for his generosity. He gave liberally to aid the needy. He shared his wealth with his family and spent money on their happiness. He spent freely to meet his own need. Nevertheless, each year his wealth increased more rapidly than he spent it.

There were certain friends from his youth who came to him and said, "You, Arkad, are more fortunate than we. You have become the richest man in Babylon while we struggle day to day. You wear the finest clothes and enjoy the most exotic foods, while we can barely put presentable clothes on our families' backs, and we struggle to feed them as best we can.

"Yet, we were once equal. We studied under the same master, played at the same games, and in neither of those did you outshine us. And in the years since, you have become no more honorable a citizen than we have. You have not worked harder than we have, or more faithfully.

"Why should a fickle fate single you out to enjoy all the good things of life and ignore us who are equally deserving?"

Arkad smiled lovingly, but reproached them. "If you have not acquired more than enough to sustain a bare existence in the years since we were youths, it is because either you have failed to learn the rules that govern the building of wealth, or you ignore them.

"'Fickle Fate' is a vicious goddess who brings no lasting good to anyone. In fact, she brings ruin to nearly all who gain wealth without earning it. They spend recklessly and are soon left with nothing except appetites and desires they cannot afford. Others whom she favors become misers and hoard their wealth, fearing to spend what they have, knowing they lack the ability to replace it. Even worse, they fear they will lose it to robbers, and doom themselves to lives of emptiness and secret misery.

"There probably are some who can take unearned gold and can be happy and content, or so I've heard. But there are so few of these men, I have yet to meet one. Look at the men who have inherited sudden wealth, and see if I do not speak the truth."

Arkad's friends admitted that his words were true. They knew some who had inherited wealth, but none who had succeeded in retaining their good fortune. They pressed Arkad to explain to them how he had become so prosperous.

"In my youth," he continued, "I looked about and saw all the good things there were to bring happiness and contentment. I realized that wealth increased the power of all these things.

"Wealth is a power. With wealth, many more things are possible. One may decorate his home with the richest furnishings. One may sail the distant seas, and feast on delicacies of faraway lands. One may buy the jewels and adornments of the gold worker and the stone polisher, and give meaningful sums to charities. One may even build mighty temples to the gods. With wealth, one may do all these things and many others that delight the senses and gratify the soul.

"When I realized this, I made a commitment that I would claim my share of the good things in this world. I would not be someone standing on the side, envious of others enjoying life. I would not be content to clothe myself in the cheapest garment that looked respectable, nor be satisfied with the lot of a poor man. On the contrary, I would make myself a guest at life's banquet.

"As you know, I am the son of a humble merchant with a large family, so there was no chance of an inheritance. And as you so frankly said, I did not have the gift of great wisdom. I realized that if I was to achieve the wealth I desired, it would require time and study.

"As for time, all men have it in abundance. Every one of you has let slip away enough time to have made yourself wealthy. Yet, you admit, you have nothing to show for it except your good families, of which you have a right to be proud.

"As for study, you will recall that our teacher taught us there are two kinds of learning: one in which we learn things and know them, and another in which we learn how to find out about things we do not know.

"Therefore, I decided to find out how to accumulate wealth and, when I had found out, to make that my task and do it well. For, is it not wise to enjoy life while we are still here to see the sun rise upon the earth each day?

"I found employment as a scribe in the hall of records, and worked hard and long each day etching clay tablets. Week after week, month after month I worked, yet I had nothing to show for my earnings. All my earnings were spent on food and clothing and penance to the gods, and other things I could not even remember. But I remained determined.

"One day Algamish, the money lender, came to the house of the city master and ordered a copy of the Ninth Law, and said to me, 'I must have this in two days. If you can complete the task in that time, I will give you two coppers.'

"So I labored hard, but the Ninth Law is long, and it was a difficult task. When Algamish returned, I had not yet finished. He was angry, and if I had been his slave he would have beaten me. But knowing the city master would not permit him to harm me, I was not afraid, so I said to Algamish, 'You are a very rich man. Tell me how I may also become rich, and I will carve the clay all night and finish before sunrise.'

"He smiled and replied, 'You are a courageous rascal, but we will call it a bargain.'

"All that night I carved, though my back was in pain and the smell of the candle made my head ache until I could barely see. Though I wanted to sleep, I persisted. And when Algamish returned at sunup, the tablets were complete.

"'Now,' I said, 'tell me what you promised.'

"'You have fulfilled your side of the bargain, my son,' he said kindly, 'and I am ready to fulfill mine. I will tell you these things you wish to know because I am becoming an old man, and an old man loves to talk. And when the young come to the aged for advice, they receive the wisdom of years. Too often they think age knows only the wisdom of days gone by, and that it is of little value today. But remember this: The sun that shines today is the sun that will shine tomorrow. It is the sun that rose when your grandfather was born, and it will still be rising after your grandchildren have passed into the hereafter.

"'The thoughts of youth,' he continued, 'are like the meteors that dazzle in the sky and then disappear, but the wisdom of age is like the stars that shine so unchanged that a sailor may depend on them to steer his ship.

"'Mark my words, for if you do not, you will fail to grasp the truth I will tell you, and you will think your night's work has been in vain.'

"Then he looked at me shrewdly from under his shaggy brows and said in a low, forceful tone, 'I found the road to wealth when I decided that a part of all that I earn was mine to keep. And so you will find it as well.'

"'Is that all?' I asked.

"'That was sufficient to turn the heart of a sheep herder into the heart of a money lender,' he replied.

"'But all I earn is mine to keep, is it not?" I demanded.

"'Far from it,' he replied. 'Do you not pay the garment maker? Do you not pay the sandal maker? Do you not pay for the things you eat? Can you live in Babylon without spending? What do you have to show for your earnings of the last month? For the past year? Fool! You pay everyone but yourself. You labor for others. You might as well be a slave and work only for what your master gives you to eat and wear.

"'Tell me this,' he said, peering at me intently. 'If you kept one-tenth of what you earn, how much would you have in ten years?'

"My knowledge of numbers did not forsake me, and I answered, 'As much as I make in one year.'

"'You speak only half the truth,' he retorted. 'Every piece of gold you save is a slave to work for you. Every copper it earns is its child that can also earn for you. If you wish to become wealthy, then the money you save must earn and its children must earn, and its children's children must earn, so that all may help to give you the abundance you crave.

"'You think I cheat you for your long night's work,' he continued, 'but I am paying you a thousand times over if you have the intelligence to understand the truth I offer you.

"'A part of all you earn is yours to keep. It should not be less than a tenth, no matter how much or how little you earn. It can be as much more as you can afford. Pay yourself first, then spend only what is left. Do not spend first. And make sure you have enough for shelter, food, and charity before you buy your fancy clothes.

"'Wealth, like a tree, grows from a tiny seed. The first copper you save is the seed from which your tree of wealth will grow. The sooner you plant that seed, the sooner the tree will grow. And the more faithfully you nourish and water that tree with consistent savings, the sooner you will bask in contentment beneath its shade.' He then took his tablets and went away.

"I thought about what he had said, and it seemed reasonable. I decided I would try it. Each time I was paid, I took one out of every ten pieces of copper and hid it away. And strange as it may seem, I was no shorter of funds than before. I noticed little difference as I managed to get along without it. Often I was tempted, as my hoard began to grow, to spend it on exotic goods displayed in the merchants' shops, brought by camels and ships from the land of the Phoenicians. But wisely I refrained.

"Twelve months after Algamish had come and gone, he returned and said to me, 'Son, have you paid yourself not less than one-tenth of all you have earned for the past year?'

"I answered proudly, 'Yes, I have!'

"'That is good,' he answered, smiling broadly. 'And what have you done with it?'

"'I have given it to Azmur, the bricklayer, who told me he knew of a place to buy rare jewels from the Phoenicians. When he returns, we will sell them at high prices and divide the earnings.'

"'Every fool must learn,' he growled, 'but why do you trust the knowledge of a bricklayer about buying jewels? Would you go to the bread maker to inquire about the stars? No, by my tunic, you would go to the astrologer, if you had the power to think. Your savings are gone, my boy, you have jerked your wealth tree up by the roots. But you are young, you can plant another. Try again. Next time if you want advice about jewels, go to the jewel merchant. If you want to know about growing crops, go to a farmer. Advice is freely given away, but take it only from those worthy to give it. If you take advice about your savings from those with no experience in such matters, you will pay with your savings, proving the hollowness of their opinions.' Saying this, he turned and went away.

"And it was as he said, for the Phoenicians are scoundrels, and sold to Azmur nothing more than colored bits of glass that looked like gems. But as Algamish had bid me, I again saved one copper out of every ten, for I had formed the habit and it was no longer difficult.

"Again, twelve months later, Algamish came to the room of the scribes and asked me, 'What progress have you made since I last saw you?'

"'I paid myself first faithfully,' I replied, 'and my savings I entrusted to Agger the shield maker, to buy bronze, and each fourth month he pays me the interest.'

"'That is good. And what do you do with this interest?'

"'I have a grand feast with honey and fine wine and spiced cake. I have bought for myself a scarlet tunic, and one day I will buy a camel upon which I can ride.'

"To which Algamish laughed. 'You eat the children of your savings? Then how do you expect them to work for you? And how can they have children that will also work for you? First get yourself an army of golden coins to work as slaves, and then you can enjoy many rich banquets without regret.' Saying this, he smiled and went away again.

"I did not see him for two years. When he returned, his face was deeply lined, for he was becoming an old man. He said to me, 'Arkad, have you achieved the wealth you dreamed of?'

"I answered, 'I have not yet achieved all the wealth I desire, but I have achieved some, and it earns more, and its earnings earn still more.'

"'And do you still take the advice of brick makers?'

"'About brick making they give expert advice!' I retorted.

"'Arkad,' he continued, 'you have learned your lessons well. You first learned to live on less than you earn, to pay yourself first. Next, you learned to seek advice from those who were qualified, through their own experience, to give it. And last, you have learned to make gold work for you.

"'You have taught yourself how to acquire money, how to keep it, and how to use it. Therefore, you are qualified to hold a responsible position. I am becoming an old man. My sons think only of spending and give no thought to saving and earning. My interests are significant, and I fear they are too much for me to look after. If you will go to Nippur and look after my lands there, I will make you my partner and you will share in my estate.'

"'So I went to Nippur and took charge of his holdings, which were large. Because I was full of ambition, and had mastered the three laws of successfully handling wealth, I was able to increase greatly the value of his properties. We both prospered much, and when the spirit of Algamish departed for the sphere of darkness, I shared in his estate as he had arranged under the law."

When Arkad had finished his story, one if his friends said, "You were indeed fortunate that Algamish made you an heir."

"I was fortunate only in that I had the desire to prosper before I first met him. For four years did I not prove my clarity of purpose by keeping one-tenth of all I earned? Would you call a fisherman lucky who, for many years, studied the habits of fish so that with each changing wind he could cast his net around them? Opportunity is a haughty goddess who wastes no time on those who are unprepared."

Arkad continued, "Therefore, do not rely on luck to save you, my friends. But there is one more thing you must have if you wish to become wealthy. Without it, you most certainly will fail. Do you know what it is? What say you?"

Each man searched the faces of the others for an answer, but found none.

Arkad broke the silence, "It is willpower!

"Willpower is the unflinching purpose to carry out a task you set for yourself, no matter what. If I set a goal, no matter how large or small, I will see it through. How else will I have confidence that I am capable of doing important things? If I said, 'For a hundred days I will walk across this bridge, pick up a pebble and throw it into the stream,' I would do it. If on the seventh day I passed by and forgot to throw one in, I would not say, 'It's only a day, tomorrow I will throw in two.' Instead, I would retrace my steps and cast the pebble. On the twentieth day I would not say, 'Arkad, this is useless. How does it serve you to throw a pebble every day? Throw in a handful and be done with it.' No, I would not say that nor do it. When I set a task for myself, I complete it."

And then another friend spoke up and said, "If what you tell us is true, and it seems to be reasonable, then if it is so simple, if all men did this there would not be enough wealth to go around."

"Wealth grows when men exert energy," Arkad replied. "If a rich man builds himself a new palace, is the gold he pays out gone? No, the brick maker has part of it, the laborer has part of it. Everyone who labors on the house has a part of it. And when the palace is complete, is it not worth all it cost? And the ground it stands on, is it not worth more? And the land next to it, is it not worth more? Wealth grows in magical ways. No man can foresee the limit of it. Have not the Phoenicians built great cities on barren coastal lands with the wealth that came from their ships of commerce on the seas?"

"What then do you suggest we do so we may also become wealthy?" asked yet another friend. "I am no longer a young man, and I have nothing set aside."

"It is true that youth is the best time to begin to grow wealth, because a coin saved by a young man has many years to grow earnings for its master. But a coin saved today is better than a coin never saved. It, too, can grow earnings for the months or years you continue to walk in the sunshine of this world. Begin to grow your wealth today, and you will soon be grateful for your good sense.

"Forming good habits is easier for the young, who are still learning to become wise and prudent men. Even so, if you aspire to develop good habits you can do so at any age. I advise you to embrace the wisdom of Algamish and say to yourself, 'A part of all I earn is mine to keep.' Say it in the morning when you first arise. Say it at noon. Say it at night. Say it every hour of the day. Say it to yourself until the words stand out like letters of fire across the sky.

"Impress this idea upon your mind. Fill yourself with this thought. Then take whatever portion seems wise, but not less than one-tenth, and set it aside. Arrange your other expenses to make this possible. But pay yourself first. Soon you will know what a rich feeling it is to own treasure that is yours alone. A new joy will thrill you. You will be inspired to put forth greater effort to earn even more. For of your increased earnings, the same percentage will also be yours to keep.

"Then learn to make your treasure work for you. Make it your slave. Make its children and its children's children work for you.

"Ensure that you will have income for your future. Look at the old men around you, and remember that the day will come when you will be one of them. Therefore, invest wisely. Promises of extraordinary earnings are tempting, but they lure the unwary into unwise decisions that lead to loss and remorse. If it sounds too good to be true, it nearly always is.

"Provide for your family so they will not be left wanting when you leave this world. It is always possible to arrange for such protection by making small payments at regular intervals. Therefore, a wise man acts accordingly and doesn't wait.

"Listen to wise men. Seek expert advice from those who have done well with money. Let them save you from trusting your money to a bricklayer buying jewels. A safe and reasonable return is better than one with a great deal of risk.

"Enjoy life while you can. Do not try to save so much that you strain your ability to be comfortable. If one-tenth of all you earn is as much as you can save, be content with that amount. Live within the rest of your earnings, but don't feel guilty about spending it. Life is good and life is rich with things worthwhile and things to enjoy."

Arkad's friends thanked him and went on their way. Some did not understand his teaching, and went away perplexed. Some mocked him because they thought that one so rich should share his wealth with old friends who were less fortunate.

But some had a new light in their eyes. They realized that Algamish had come back again and again to the room of the scribes because he was watching a man work his way out of darkness into light, and he knew he had a place for that man when he had found that light. But Algamish realized that no one could step into that opportunity until he was ready for it, having fully attained his own understanding.

These latter friends were the ones who, in the following years, frequently revisited Arkad, who was glad to see them. He counseled with them and freely shared his wisdom with them, as caring men do. He helped them invest their savings wisely, so it would earn a reasonable return with safety, not exceeding a smart level of risk.

The turning point in these men's lives came on the day they realized that the truth that had come from Algamish to Arkad had come from Arkad to them.

A PART OF ALL YOU EARN
IS YOURS TO KEEP.

CHAPTER EIGHT

Seven Cures for a Lean Purse

The glory of Babylon endures. Across the millennia its reputation stands as one of the richest of cities, with an abundance of fabulous treasures.

Yet that was not always the case. The riches of Babylon were made possible by the wisdom of its people, and their ability to apply the principles of wealth. But first they had to learn those principles.

Around 2800 BC, King Sargon returned to Babylon after defeating the Elamites and was confronted with a serious situation. The royal chancellor explained it to the king this way:

"Because of you, King, Babylon has seen many years of prosperity. You built the great irrigation canals and the mighty temples of the gods. But now that these works are completed, many citizens are unable to support themselves. The laborers have no work. The merchants have few customers. The people have little gold to buy food, so the farmers cannot sell their produce."

"But what has happened to all the gold that we spent for these great improvements?" demanded the king.

"I fear it has found its way into the hands of a very few rich men in our city," responded the chancellor. "It filtered through the fingers of most of our people as quickly as goat's milk through a strainer. Now that the stream of gold has ceased to flow, most of our people have nothing to show for their earnings."

The king was thoughtful for some time. Then he asked, "Why should so few men be able to acquire all the gold?"

"Because they know how," replied the chancellor. "They must not be condemned for succeeding because they know how. It would also be unjust to take from a man what he has earned fairly, to give to men of less ability."

"But," asked the king, "should not all people be able to learn how to accumulate gold and therefore become rich and prosperous themselves?"

"Quite possibly, your excellency. But who can teach them? Certainly not the priests, because they know nothing of how to accumulate wealth."

"Who knows best, in all our city, how to become wealthy, Chancellor?" asked the king.

"It is a question that answers itself, your majesty. Who has amassed the greatest wealth in Babylon?"

"Well said, my able chancellor. It is Arkad. He is the richest man in Babylon. Bring him to me tomorrow."

The next day, Arkad presented himself to the king. He stood straight and spry, even at the age of 70.

"Arkad," spoke the king, "is it true that you are the richest man in Babylon?"

"So it is reported, your majesty, and it is my understanding that no man disputes it."

"How did you become so wealthy?"

"By taking advantage of opportunities available to all citizens of our great city."

"And you started with nothing?" asked the king.

"Only a great desire for wealth. Besides this, I had nothing."

"Arkad," continued the king, "Our city is in a very unhappy state. Only a few men know how to acquire wealth, and therefore all the wealth is theirs, while most of our citizens lack the knowledge of how to keep any part of the gold they receive.

"It is my desire that Babylon will be the greatest and wealthiest city in the world. But that is only possible if it is a city of many wealthy men. Therefore, I believe we must teach all the people how to acquire riches. Tell me, Arkad, is there any secret to acquiring wealth? Can it be taught?"

"I believe it can, good king. That which one man knows can be taught to others. I myself was once a poor man, uneducated in the ways of acquiring wealth. Others can learn just as I did."

The king's eyes glowed. "Arkad, you speak the words I wish to hear. Will you join me in this noble cause? Will you teach this knowledge at a school for teachers, who will in turn teach other teachers, until there are enough trained to teach these truths to everyone in this city who wants to learn?"

Arkad bowed and said, "I am your humble servant. Whatever knowledge I possess I will gladly share for the betterment of my fellow men and the glory of my king.

"Let your good chancellor arrange for me a class of one hundred men, and I will teach them the seven cures that fattened my purse when it was the leanest in all of Babylon."

Fourteen days later, as the king had commanded, one hundred chosen men gathered in a semicircle in the great hall of the Temple of Learning. Arkad sat beside a small table, where incense burned in a sacred lamp.

"There he is," whispered one student as he nudged his neighbor, "the richest man in Babylon. He is only a man, no different from the rest of us."

"As a dutiful subject of our great king," Arkad began, "I stand before you in his service. Because I was once a poor youth who greatly desired gold, and because I found knowledge that enabled me to acquire it, our king has asked that I share that knowledge with you, so that you may share it with others.

"I started in the humblest way, with no advantage not shared by you and every citizen of Babylon. I loathed the useless emptiness of my purse. I wanted it to be round and full, clinking with the sound of gold. Therefore, I sought every remedy for a lean purse. I found seven.

"To all of you assembled here, I shall explain these seven cures for a lean purse, which I recommend to all who wish to acquire much gold. Each day for seven days I will explain to you one of the seven remedies.

"Listen carefully to the knowledge I will share. Debate it with me. Discuss it among yourselves. Learn these lessons thoroughly so that you may also plant the seeds of wealth in your own purse. First, each of you must begin wisely to build a fortune of your own. Then, and only then, will you be competent to teach these truths to others.

"I will teach you in simple terms how to fatten your purses. This is the first step leading to the temple of wealth, and no man can climb without planting his feet firmly upon the first step.

"Let us now consider the first cure."

The First Cure
BEGIN BY FATTENING YOUR PURSE

Arkad addressed a thoughtful man in the second row. "My good friend, what kind of work do you do?"

"I am a scribe," said the man. "I carve records upon the clay tablets."

"That is precisely the work I was doing when I earned my first coppers," said Arkad. "Therefore, you have the same opportunity to build a fortune."

He next spoke to a ruddy-faced man near the back of the hall. "And how do you earn your living?" he asked.

The man stood up with a smile on his lips and pride in his face. "I am a baker," he said. "I make honey cakes to sweeten the days of hard-working men in our fair city."

"That is good. Because you work and earn an income, you have every opportunity to succeed that I had."

Arkad proceeded to ask each man how he earned his living. When he had finished questioning them, he said, "As you see, there are many trades and many kinds of work by which men may earn coins. Each provides a stream of gold that may be large or small, depending on the job and the abilities of the laborer. Regardless of the amount, the coins you earn as a result of your labor flow into your own purse. Is that not true?"

They nodded in agreement.

"Then wouldn't you agree that, if you wish to build wealth for yourself, it is wise to begin by utilizing the source of wealth you have already established?"

Again, they agreed.

Then Arkad turned to a humble man who had declared himself an egg merchant. "If you place ten eggs in your best basket every morning, and every evening take out nine eggs, what will eventually happen?"

"In time the basket will overflow."

"Correct. Why?"

"Because each day I put in one more egg than I take out."

Arkad turned to the class with a smile. "Does any man here have a lean purse?"

First they looked amused. Then they all laughed. Finally they waved their empty purses in jest.

"Alright. Then I will tell you the first remedy I learned to cure a lean purse. Do exactly as I have suggested to the egg merchant. For every ten coins you place in your purse, spend only nine. Your purse will quickly become fatter, and its increasing weight will feel good in your hand and bring satisfaction to your soul.

"Do not scoff at what I say because it sounds so simple. Truth is always simple. I told you I would tell you how I built my fortune. This was my beginning. I, too, carried a lean purse and cursed it because there were not enough coins in it to satisfy my desires. I wanted more than my income and wealth could provide. When I started to spend only nine coins out of every ten I made, my purse became fatter as I began to accumulate wealth. So will yours.

"Now I will share a strange truth, one I cannot explain. When I began to spend only nine-tenths of what I made, I managed to get along just as well as before. I was no less able to buy the things I needed. Also, before long, coins seemed to come to me more easily than before. I cannot tell you how or why, but they did. Surely it must be a law of the gods that, when a man saves for himself some portion of his earnings, gold will come to him more easily. Whether the gods play a role or not, I can tell you I have known this strange phenomenon to be real: When you begin to accumulate wealth, good things come your way. But when your purse is empty, gold seems to stay far away, while bad things lie in wait around every bend in the road.

"Which do you desire the most? Is it the gratification of your desires in this moment? A jewel, a more elegant robe, more food...things that are soon gone and forgotten? Or do you desire more substantial belongings, like gold, land, herds, merchandise, investments that will grow in value and bring more income? The nine coins you spend today will satisfy your desires of the moment. The one you leave in your purse will bring you wealth that grows.

"This, my students, is the first remedy I discovered to cure my lean purse, and it will cure yours. For every ten coins you put in, spend only nine.

"Question me, if you like. Debate this among yourselves. If any man can prove it is untrue, tell me tomorrow when we meet again."

The Second Cure
Control Your Expenses

On the second day of teaching, Arkad took his place at the front of the class. He began, "My friends, some of you have asked how a man can save one out of every ten coins he earns, when all ten coins are not enough to cover his necessary expenses."

He began his answer with a question. "Yesterday, how many of you carried lean purses?"

"All of us," answered the class.

Arkad nodded. "And yet," he said, "you do not all earn the same amount. Some earn more than others. Some of you have larger families to support. But all of your purses are equally lean. I will share with you a truth about most men. What each of us sees as 'necessary' expenses will increase to equal our income, unless we do something about it.

"Do not confuse necessary expenses with desires. Every one of you, with your good family, has more desires than your earnings can fulfill. Your earnings are spent to fulfill those desires as far as they will go. Yet no matter how much you buy and accumulate, you have even more desires that remain unmet.

"All men, young and old, have more desires than they can satisfy. Just because I am very wealthy, do you think I can satisfy all my desires? I assure you, I cannot. There are limits to my time, to my strength. There are limits to the distance I can travel, and to what I can eat. There are limits to the zest with which I can enjoy the bounties of this world. And yes, there is a limit to my wealth.

"Just as the weeds in your garden will take over if you leave space for them to flourish, your desires, too, will grow freely as long as there is a possibility they will be fulfilled. Your desires are unlimited, but you can gratify only a few.

"Study carefully the way of life you have become accustomed to. That is where you will find expenses that you have called 'necessary,' but that in reality may be desires. Those are expenses that may wisely be reduced or eliminated. Spend wisely. Enjoy your purchases, and make it your goal to demand one hundred percent value for every coin you spend.

"Therefore, engrave upon the clay a list of expenditures you would like to make. Select those that are truly necessary and others you can pay for with nine-tenths of your income. Cross out the rest, consider them as part of that great multitude of desires that must go unsatisfied—then have no regrets. Spend only that amount that is accounted for in your spending plan, and keep a dollar for every ten you earn.

"Do not touch the one-tenth that is fattening your purse. Let that be the great desire that is indeed being fulfilled. Keep working with your list of expenses, keep adjusting it as needed. Let it help you protect the growing wealth in your purse."

One student, wearing a robe of red and gold, stood up and said, "I am a free man. I believe it is my right to enjoy the good things of life. Therefore I rebel against the slavery of a budget that determines how much I may spend and for what. I feel it would take much pleasure from my life, and make me little more than a pack mule carrying a burden."

Arkad replied, "Who, my friend, would determine your spending plan?"

"I would, of course," responded the protesting student.

"In that case, if a pack mule were to plan his burden, would he include jewels and rugs and heavy bars of gold? He would not. He would include hay and grain and a bag of water for the desert trail.

"The purpose of a spending plan is to help you fatten your purse. It is to assist you in having the coins to pay for necessities and, as much as your income allows, your other desires. It is to enable you to fulfill your most cherished desires by defending them from your casual wishes. It is like a bright light in a dark cave that shows you the leaks in your purse so you can stop them, and control your expenditures so they are used to fulfill those desires that are most important to you.

"This, then is the second cure for a lean purse. Have a spending plan so you can have coins to pay for necessities and for your enjoyments, and to fulfill your worthwhile desires without spending more than nine-tenths of your earnings."

The Third Cure
Make Your Gold Multiply

"Behold, your purse is becoming fatter. You have disciplined yourself to leave one coin in your purse for every ten you earn. You have controlled your expenditures to protect your growing treasure. Next, we will consider ways to put your treasure to work so that it may earn yet more treasure. Gold in your purse is gratifying, but it earns nothing for you. The gold you retain from your earnings is only the beginning. The earnings it will make will build your fortune." These were Arkad's words to his class on the third day of their meeting.

"How, then, might we put our gold to work?

"My first investment was unfortunate, for I lost it all, a tale I will share on another day. My first profitable investment was a loan I made to a man named Aggar, a shield maker. Every year he bought a large shipment of bronze brought from across the sea to use in his trade. Since he did not have the large amount of capital required to pay the merchants, he would borrow from those of us who had extra coins. He was an honorable man. He repaid every loan, together with a generous amount of interest, as he sold his well-made shields.

"Each time I loaned to him, I also loaned back the interest he had paid to me. In that way, not only did my capital increase, but its earnings also increased. It was most gratifying to have those sums return every year to my purse.

"I tell you, my students, a man's wealth is not in the coins he carries in his purse; it is the income he builds, the golden stream that continually flows into his purse and keeps it forever bulging. That is what every man desires. That is what you, each one of you, desires—an income that continues to come whether you work hard from sunrise to sunset or enjoy your leisure.

"I have acquired great income, so great that I am called a very rich man. My loans to Aggar were my first training in profitable investing. As I gained wisdom from that experience, and as my capital increased, I extended my loans and investments. From a few sources at first and from many sources later, a golden stream of wealth flowed and continues to flow into my purse, available for me to use for any wise and desirable purposes I choose.

"Behold, from my humble earnings I had acquired a purse full of gold coins, or I would say a hoard of golden slaves, each laboring and earning more gold. As they labored for me, so their children also labored and their children's children, until their combined efforts produced great income for my enrichment.

"Gold increases rapidly when making reasonable earnings, as you will see from this tale of a farmer and his firstborn son.

"When the child was born, the farmer took ten pieces of silver to a money lender and asked him to keep it on loan for the boy until he reached the age of twenty. The money lender did as the farmer asked, and agreed to pay interest on the silver in the amount of one-fourth of its value every four years. Because the farmer wanted the sum to be held for his son for twenty years, he instructed the money lender to add the interest to the principle every year, so that in each year that followed, the interest payment would be one-fourth the value of the ten pieces of silver as well as the amount of interest already paid.

"When the boy had reached the age of twenty years, the farmer again went to the money lender to inquire about the silver. The money lender explained that because this sum had been increased by compound interest, the original ten pieces of silver had now grown to thirty and one-half pieces.

"The farmer was well pleased, and because the son did not need the coins, he left them with the money lender. When the son became fifty years of age, and his father had passed to the other world, the money lender paid the son in settlement one hundred and sixty-seven pieces of silver.

"In fifty years, the investment had earned compounded interest and had thus multiplied itself almost seventeen times.

"This, then, is the third cure for a lean purse: Put your money to work for you so it will make money and continue to compound. A stream of wealth will continue to grow for you night and day."

The Fourth Cure
Guard Your Treasures from Loss

On the fourth day, Arkad told his class, "Misfortune loves a shining mark. Gold in a man's purse must be guarded closely, or it will be lost. Thus it is wise to first secure small amounts and learn to protect them before the gods entrust us with more.

"Every owner of gold is tempted by opportunities that appear to offer large sums in return for investing in what seem to be reasonable projects. Often friends and relatives are eagerly entering into such investments, and urge him to follow.

"The first sound principle of investment is security for your principle. Is it wise to be enticed by larger earnings when your principle may be lost? I say it is not. If you take unreasonable risks with your gold, you are likely to pay the penalty of losing your investment. Before you part with your treasure, study carefully each assurance that it will be repaid. Do not be misled by your own romantic desires to make wealth rapidly.

"Before you loan it to any man, make sure he has the ability to repay and a reputation for doing so, and thereby avoid making him a gift of your hard-earned treasure.

"Before you invest in any area, know the dangers that may be lurking.

"My own first investment was a tragedy to me at the time. I diligently saved coins for a year, then entrusted them to a brickmaker named Azmur, who was traveling across the sea to buy jewels from the Phoenicians. We were to sell the jewels upon his return and divide the profits. The Phoenicians were scoundrels and sold him bits of glass. My treasure was lost. Today, my experience would tell me at once that it is foolish to entrust a brickmaker to buy jewels.

"Therefore, I share with you the wisdom of my experience. Do not be too confident in your wisdom about the possible pitfalls of investments. Better by far to consult the wisdom of those with experience in handling money for profit. Such advice may well have a value equal to that of your investment if it keeps you from losing it.

"This, then, is the fourth cure for a lean purse, and is of great importance if it prevents you from losing your treasure once you have earned it. Guard your wealth from loss by investing only where your principle is safe, where it may be reclaimed if you wish, and where you will not fail to collect fair earnings on your investment. Consult with wise men. Secure the advice of those experienced in the profitable handling of gold. Let their wisdom protect you from unsafe investments."

The Fifth Cure
Make Your Home a Profitable Investment

"If a man sets aside nine-tenths of his earnings to live on and enjoy life, and if he can turn a portion of that nine-tenths into a profitable investment with no detriment to his well-being, then his wealth will grow much faster." So spoke Arkad to his class at their fifth lesson.

"Too many men in Babylon raise their families in unsuitable dwellings. They pay high rents to exacting landlords for rooms where their wives have no patch of land to raise the blooms that gladden a woman's heart, and their children have no place to play except in unclean alleys. No man's family can fully enjoy life unless they have a plot of clean earth where their children can play, and where the wife may raise blossoms and good, rich herbs to feed her family.

"It brings gladness to a man's heart to eat the figs from his own trees and the grapes of his own vines. To own his own home, and to have it be a place he is proud to care for, puts confidence in his heart and greater effort behind all his endeavors. Therefore, I recommend that every man own the roof that shelters him and those he loves.

"It is not beyond the ability of any well-intentioned man to own his own home. Has not our great king extended the walls of Babylon so widely that, within them, much land is now unused and may be purchased at reasonable sums?

"Also, I say to you, my students, that the money lenders gladly consider the desires of men who seek homes and land for their families. With little difficulty you may borrow to pay the brickmaker and the builder for such commendable purposes, if you can show a reasonable sum that you yourself have provided for the purpose. Then, when the house is built, you can pay the money lender with the same regularity that you paid the landlord. And since each payment will reduce your debt to the money lender, in a few years you will have repaid his loan.

"Then your heart will be glad because you will own in your own right a valuable property, and your only cost will be the king's taxes.

"The heart of your good wife will also be glad, and she will go more often to the river to wash your robes, so that she may each time return with a goatskin of water to pour upon her growing garden.

"As you will see, many blessings come to the man who owns his own home. It greatly reduces his cost of living, making more of his earnings available for pleasures and the fulfillment of his desires. This, then, is the fifth cure for a lean purse. Own your home."

The Sixth Cure
Ensure a Future Income

"The life of every man proceeds from his childhood to his old age. This is the path of life, and no man may deviate from it unless the gods call him prematurely to the world beyond. Therefore, it is a man's duty to make preparations for a suitable income in the days to come, when he is no longer young, and to make preparations for his family should he no longer be with them to comfort and support them. This lesson will instruct you in how to provide a full purse when time has made you less able to earn." So Arkad addressed his class on the sixth day.

"The man who, because of his understanding of the laws of wealth, acquires a surplus of treasure, should give thought to those future days. He should make certain investments or provisions that will sustain themselves and be safe for many years, and be available when the time he has wisely anticipated arrives.

"There are many ways for a man to provide safely for his future. He could bury treasure in a secret hiding place but, even if hidden with great skill, it might still be found and stolen by thieves. For this reason I do not recommend this plan.

"Instead, a man may buy houses or lands for this purpose, choosing wisely for their usefulness and value in the future. Such properties have permanent value, and their rental or sale will provide well for this purpose.

"A man might also loan a small sum to the money lender and increase it at regular intervals. The interest the money lender adds to the sum will greatly increase its value. Not long ago the sandal maker, Ansan, told me that each week for eight years he had deposited two pieces of silver with his money lender, who had recently given him an accounting over which Ansan greatly rejoiced. The total of his small deposits and the interest paid had now become a thousand and forty pieces of silver.

"I gladly encouraged Ansan by demonstrating that in twelve years more, if he continues his regular deposits of just two pieces of silver each week, the money lender would then owe him four thousand pieces of silver, a worthy sum to provide for him and his family for the rest of his life.

"Surely, when such small, regular payments produce such profitable results, no man can afford not to ensure a treasure for his old age and the protection of his family, no matter how prosperous his business and his investments may be.

"I would like to say more about this. It is my belief that one day, wise-thinking men will devise a plan to insure against death, whereby many men make very small, regular payments, and the aggregate amount provides a handsome sum for the family of each member who passes to the dark beyond. The plan and its management must be as stable as the king's throne. I see this as something desirable, something I could recommend heartily. Today it is not possible, but I feel someday such a plan will come to pass and be a great blessing to many men, because even the first small payment will make a snug fortune available for a member's family if he should pass on.

"Because we live in our own day, each of us must make use of the means available now to accomplish our purposes. Therefore I urge every man to ensure he does not carry a lean purse in his mature years, for a lean purse is a terrible tragedy for a man no longer able to earn or a family with no provider.

"This, then, is the sixth cure for a lean purse. Provide in advance for your needs as you age and for the protection of your family."

The Seventh Cure
Increase Your Ability to Earn

At last Arkad addressed his class on the seventh day. "Today I speak to you, my students, of one of the most vital remedies for a lean purse. I will speak not of gold but of yourselves, of the men beneath the robes of many colors who sit before me. I will talk of things that exist within the minds and lives of men, things that work for or against their success.

"Not long ago, a young man came to me seeking to borrow. When I asked the reason for his need, he complained that his earnings were insufficient to pay his expenses. I explained to him that, in such circumstances, he was a poor customer for a money lender since he lacked surplus earnings to repay the loan.

"'What you need, young man,' I told him, 'is to earn more coins. What are you doing to increase your earning capacity?'

"'I've done all I can,' he replied. 'Six times within two moons I have approached my master to ask that my pay be increased, but without success. No man can ask more often than that.'"

"We, here, may smile at his simplicity, yet he did possess one of the vital requirements to increase his earnings. Within him was a strong desire to earn more, a proper and commendable desire.

"Accomplishments are the fruits of desire. If you wish to accomplish much, your desires must be strong and specific. Vague desires are nothing more than weak longings. For a man to wish to be rich is of little use. But if a man desires five pieces of gold, he has a tangible desire that he can pursue to fulfillment. When he backs that desire for five pieces of gold with the strength and means to secure it, he can then apply similar methods to obtain ten and then twenty pieces of gold, and later a thousand pieces and, behold, he has become wealthy. In learning to secure his one small, specific desire, he has trained himself to secure a larger one. This is the process by which wealth is accumulated: first in small sums, then in larger ones as a man learns and becomes more capable.

"Desires must be simple and specific. They defeat their own purpose if there are too many of them, or if they are confusing or beyond a man's training to accomplish.

"As a man becomes proficient in his chosen profession, his ability to earn will increase. In those days when I was a humble scribe carving upon the clay for a few coppers each day, I observed that other workers did more and were paid more. Therefore, I determined that I would be exceeded by none. It did not take long for me to discover the reason for their greater success. With more interest in my work, more concentration on my task, and more persistence in my effort, behold, few men could carve more tablets in a day than I. My increased skill was promptly rewarded, with no need for me to go to my master six times to ask for recognition.

"The more knowledge we have, the more we may earn. He who seeks to learn more of his profession will be richly rewarded. If he is a craftsman, he may seek to learn the methods and the tools of those most skillful in the same trade. If he works at the law or at healing, he may consult and exchange knowledge with others of his calling. If he is a merchant, he may continually seek better goods that can be purchased at lower prices.

"The affairs of mankind change and improve because keen-minded men seek greater skill, so they may better meet the needs of those they serve and with whom they trade.

"There are many things that can make a man's life rich with rewarding experiences. The following are some of those, which a man must do if he respects himself:

"He must pay his debts as promptly as he possibly can, and not purchase goods he is unable to pay for.

"He must take care of his family so they may hold him in high esteem.

"He must make a will of record that, in case the gods call him, his property may be properly and honorably divided.

"He must have compassion for those who are injured and struck by misfortune, and assist them within reasonable limits.

"He must perform thoughtful deeds for those who are dear to him.

"Thus the seventh and last cure for a lean purse is to cultivate the power of your desires, study and become wiser and more skillful, and act in such a way that you will respect yourself.

"These, then, are the seven cures for a lean purse, which, based on my experience throughout a long and successful life, I urge for all men who desire wealth," said Arkad as he prepared to say farewell to his class.

"There is more gold in Babylon, my students, than you can dream of. There is abundance for all. Go forth and practice these truths so you may prosper and grow wealthy, as is your right.

"Do not keep this knowledge to yourself. Go forth and teach these truths so that every honorable subject of his majesty may also share liberally in the ample wealth of our beloved city."

CHAPTER NINE

THE FIVE LAWS OF GOLD

The elderly merchant, Kalabab, looked around him at the young men watching intently as he spoke. "If you had a choice between a bag heavy with gold or a clay tablet carved with words of wisdom, what would you choose?" he asked.

By the flickering light of desert shrubs, the suntanned faces of the listeners gleamed with interest. All 27 of the men chimed in, "The gold! The gold!"

Kalabab smiled knowingly. "Hark," he went on, raising his hand. "Hear the wild dogs out there in the night. They howl and wail because they are lean with hunger. But if you feed them, what will they do? They will fight and strut, and then fight and strut some more, giving no thought to tomorrow when they will be hungry again.

"And so it is with the sons of men. Given a choice between gold and wisdom, what do they do? They choose the gold. But when they ignore wisdom, the gold is soon wasted. Tomorrow they will wail because they have no more gold.

"Gold is reserved for those who know its laws and abide by them."

Kalabab drew his white robe close about his lean legs, for a cool night wind was blowing. Above in a canopy of blue, the stars shone brightly in the crystal clear skies of Babylonia. Behind the group loomed their faded tents tightly staked against possible desert storms. Beside the tents were neatly stacked bales of merchandise covered with skins. Nearby the camel herd sprawled in the sand, some chewing their cuds contentedly, others snoring in hoarse discord.

"Because you have served me faithfully on our long journey, because you cared well for my camels, because you toiled without complaint across the hot sands of the desert, because you fought bravely against the robbers who sought to steal my merchandise, I will tell you this night the tale of the five laws of gold, a tale the likes of which you have never heard before.

"Listen closely, with deep attention to the words I speak, for if you understand their meaning and take notice of the lessons they teach, in the days to come you will have vast amounts of gold."

He paused, drawing the interest of each man deeper with each passing moment.

The chief camel tender spoke up. "You have told us many good tales, Kalabab. We look to your wisdom to guide us after we part ways tomorrow, when our service with you will come to an end."

"Until now, I have only told you of my adventures in strange and distant lands," responded Kalabab. "But tonight I shall tell you of the wisdom of Arkad, the wise rich man."

"We have heard much about him," acknowledged the chief tender, "for he was the richest man who ever lived in Babylon."

"The richest man he was indeed, and he became so because he was wise in the ways of gold, even as no man before him had been. This night I shall tell you of his great wisdom as it was told to me by Nomasir, his son, many years ago in Nineveh, when I was only a lad.

"My master and I had lingered long into the night in the palace of Nomasir. I had helped my master bring great bundles of fine rugs, each one to be tried by Nomasir until his choice of colors was satisfied. At last he was well pleased, and commanded us to sit with him and to drink a rare wine, fragrant to the nostrils and warming to my stomach, which was unaccustomed to such a drink.

"It was then that he told us this tale of the great wisdom of Arkad, his father, even as I shall tell it to you now."

Kalabab drew another robe around his narrow shoulders to warm him as he began his tale.

"In Babylon it is the custom, as you know, that the sons of wealthy fathers live with their parents in expectation of inheriting the estate. Arkad did not approve of this custom. Therefore, when Nomasir reached the threshold of manhood, Arkad sent for him and addressed him:

"'My son, it is my desire that you succeed me as master of my estate. However, you must first prove that you are capable of handling it wisely. Therefore, I would like you to go out into the world and demonstrate your ability to acquire gold and to make yourself respected among men.

"'So that you may start well, I will give you two things that I myself lacked when I started as a poor youth to build a fortune.

"'First, I give you this bag of gold. If you use it wisely, it will be the basis of your future success.

"'Second, I give you this clay tablet upon which are carved the five laws of gold. If you simply apply them to your own thoughts and actions, they will bring you competence and security.

"'Ten years from this day, come back to the house of your father and give an account of yourself. If you prove worthy, I will make you the heir to my estate. Otherwise, I will give it to the priests so they may barter with the gods, the land in exchange for a safe journey for my soul.'

"So Nomasir went forth to make his own way, taking his bag of gold, the clay tablet carefully wrapped in silken cloth, his slave, and the horses upon which they rode.

"The ten years passed, and Nomasir, as he had agreed, returned to the house of his father who provided a great feast in his honor, and invited many friends and relatives to join in the celebration. After the feast was over, the father and mother mounted their throne-like seats at one side of the great hall. Nomasir then stood before them to give an account of himself, as he had promised his father he would.

"It was evening. The room was hazy with smoke from the wicks of the oil lamps that cast their dim light on the faces of the guests. Slaves in white woven jackets and tunics fanned the humid air rhythmically with long-stemmed palm leaves. A stately dignity colored the scene. The wife of Nomasir and his two young sons sat on rugs behind him, with friends and other members of the family gathered close by. All were eager listeners.

"'My father,' began Nomasir, 'I bow before your wisdom. Ten years ago when I stood at the gates of manhood, you bade me go forth and become a man among men, instead of remaining an idle heir to your fortune. You gave me liberally of your gold. You gave me liberally of your wisdom.

"'Of the gold, alas! I must confess to handling it disastrously. It fled, indeed, from my inexperienced hands as a wild hare flees at the first opportunity from the youth who captures him.'

"The father smiled indulgently. 'Please continue, my son, Your tale interests me in all its details.'

"'I decided to go to Ninevah,' Nomasir went on, 'as I knew it to be a growing city, and I believed I might find opportunities there. I joined a caravan and made many friends from among its members. They included two well-spoken men who had a beautiful white horse as fleet as the wind.

"'As we traveled, they told me in confidence about a wealthy man in Nineveh who owned a horse so swift that he had never been beaten. His owner believed that no other living horse could run with greater speed. Therefore, the man would wager any sum, however large, that his horse could outrun any other in all of Babylonia. My friends insisted that, compared to their horse, he was nothing more than a lumbering mule who could be beaten with ease.

"'They offered, as a great favor, to permit me to join them in a wager. I was quite carried away with the plan.

"'I'm quite sure you will not be surprised, my father, to learn that our horse was badly beaten and I lost much of my gold.'

"The father laughed.

"'Later I discovered that these men routinely traveled with caravans seeking victims for this deceitful plan. You see, the man in Nineveh was their partner and shared with them the winnings from the bets he won. This shrewd deceit taught me my first lesson in looking out for myself.

"'I was soon to learn another equally bitter lesson. In the caravan was another young man with whom I became quite friendly. He was the son of wealthy parents and, like myself, traveling to Nineveh in search of opportunity. Not long after our arrival there, he told me that a merchant had died, and his shop with its rich merchandise and customers could be bought at a minimal price. He suggested we become equal partners in the venture, but first he must return to Babylon to secure his gold. He urged me to promptly make the purchase, with the assurance that his gold would be used later to operate and maintain the shop. I did as he suggested.

"'For many moons he delayed his trip to Babylon, and in the meantime proved to be an unwise buyer and a foolish spender. I finally severed our partnership, but not before the business had deteriorated to where we had only unsellable merchandise and no money to replenish our stock. I sold what remained for a pitiful sum.

"'I tell you, my father, bitter days soon followed. I sought employment but found none, for I had no trade or training to offer an employer. I sold my horses. I sold my slave. I sold my extra robes so I might have food and a place to sleep. But each day the grim reality of loss and failure and poverty lurked closer.

"'But even in those bitter days, I remembered your confidence in me, my father. You had sent me out into the world to become a man, and I was determined to accomplish that.'

"Nomasir's mother buried her face and wept softly.

"'It was in that dark time that I thought of the tablet you had given me, on which you had carved the five laws of gold. I began at once to read most carefully your words of wisdom, and realized that if only I had sought wisdom first, my gold would not have been lost to me. I learned each law by heart, and vowed that when the goddess of good fortune smiled on me once again, I would be guided by the wisdom of age and not by the inexperience of youth.

"'For the benefit of all of you seated here this night, I will read the wisdom of my father as it was engraved upon the clay tablet, which he gave me ten years ago:

THE FIVE LAWS OF GOLD

I. Gold comes gladly and in increasing quantity to any man who will save not less than one-tenth of his earnings to create an estate for his future and that of his family.

II. Gold labors diligently and contentedly for the wise owner who finds profitable employment for it, so it can multiply as prolifically as the flocks in the field.

III. Gold clings to the protection of the cautious owner who invests it under the guidance of wise and trustworthy advisors who know well how to handle it prudently.

IV. Gold slips away from the man who invests it in businesses or purposes he does not know well, or that are not approved by those with skill in investing.

V. Gold flees the man who attempts to force it to provide impossible earnings, or who follows the alluring advice of tricksters and schemers, or who trusts it to his own inexperience and romantic investment illusions.

"'These are the five laws of gold written by my father. I now proclaim they are of greater value than gold itself, as I will show by the continuance of my tale.'

"He turned to his father. 'I have told you of the depth of poverty and despair to which my inexperience brought me. However, there is no chain of disaster that will not come to an end. Mine came when I secured employment managing slaves working upon the new wall of the city.

"'Profiting from my knowledge of the first law of gold, I saved a copper from my first earnings, adding to it at every opportunity until I had a piece of silver, and continued until one day at last I had a single piece of gold. It was a slow process, for one must spend coins to live. But I spent grudgingly, because I was determined to earn back as much gold as you had given me, my father, before the ten years were over.

"'One day the slave master, who had become a friend, said to me, "You are a thrifty youth who does not spend his earnings foolishly. Do you have gold you have saved that has not been invested?"

"'"Yes," I replied. "It is my greatest desire to accumulate gold to replace that which my father gave to me and which I have lost."

"'"It is a worthy ambition, I agree. And do you know that the gold you have saved can work for you and earn much more gold?"

"'"Alas!" I exclaimed. "My experience has been bitter, for my father's gold has fled from me, and I am in great fear that my own will do the same."

"'The slave master nodded, and said, "If you have confidence in me, I will give you a lesson in the proper handling of gold. Within a year, the outer wall will be complete and ready for the great gates of bronze that will be built at each entrance to protect the city from the king's enemies. In all Nineveh there is not enough metal to make these gates, and the king has not thought to provide it. Here is my plan: A group of us will pool our gold and send a caravan to the mines of copper and tin, which are far away, and bring the metal for the gates to Nineveh. When the king says, 'Make the great gates,' we alone will be able to supply the metal, and he will pay a rich price. If the king will not buy from us, we will yet have the metal, which we will be able to sell for a fair price."

"'In his offer I recognized an opportunity to abide by the third law of gold and invest my savings under the guidance of wise men. I was not disappointed. Our venture was a success, and my small store of gold was greatly increased by the transaction.

"'In due time, I was accepted as a member of this same group in other ventures. These men were wise in the profitable handling of gold. They discussed each prospective plan with great care before accepting it. They would take no chance on losing their principal or tying it up in unprofitable investments from which their gold could not be recovered. They would have given scant consideration to such foolish things as the horse race or the partnership into which I had entered with my lack of experience. These wise men would have immediately pointed out their weaknesses.

"'Through my association with these men, I learned to invest gold safely to bring profitable returns. As the years went on, my treasure increased more and more rapidly. I not only made back as much as I lost, but much more.

"'Through my misfortunes, my trials, and my success, time and again I have tested the wisdom of the five laws of gold, my father, and I have proven them true in every test. For the man who does not have knowledge of the five laws, gold does not come freely and it goes away quickly. But to him who abides by the five laws, gold comes and works as his dutiful slave.'

"Nomasir stopped speaking and motioned to a slave in the back of the room. The slave brought forward, one at a time, three heavy leather bags. Nomasir picked up one of these and placed it upon the floor in front of his father, then addressed him again:

"'Father, you gave to me a bag of gold, Babylon gold. Behold in its place, I return to you a bag of Nineveh gold of equal weight. An equal exchange, as all will agree.

"'You gave to me a clay tablet inscribed with wisdom. Behold, in its place, I return to you two bags of gold.' As he spoke, he took the other two bags and, again, placed them upon the floor in front of his father.

"'I do this, father, to prove to you how much greater I value your wisdom than your gold. And yet, who can measure, in bags of gold, the value of wisdom? Without wisdom, gold is quickly lost by those who have it. But with wisdom, gold can be secured by those who do not have it, as these three bags of gold prove.

"'It does, indeed, give me the deepest satisfaction, my father, to stand before you and say that, because of your wisdom, I have been able to become rich and respected before men.'

"The father rose from his chair and placed his hand fondly upon the head of Nomasir. 'You have learned your lessons well, and I am indeed fortunate to have a son to whom I may entrust my wealth.'"

Kalabab ended his tale and looked critically at his listeners.

"What does this mean to you, this tale of Nomasir?" he asked. "Who amongst you can go to your father or to the father of your wife and give an account of wise handling of his earnings? What would those honorable men think if you were to say, 'I have traveled much and learned much and labored much and earned much, yet alas, I have little gold. Some I spent wisely, some I spent foolishly, and much I lost in unwise ways.'

"Do you still think it is nothing more than the inconsistency of fate that some men have much gold and others have none? Then you're mistaken.

"Men have much gold when they know the five laws of gold and abide by them. I did not accumulate my wealth by some strange magic. I have become a wealthy merchant because I learned these five laws in my youth and abided by them.

"Wealth that comes quickly leaves quickly. Wealth that stays to give enjoyment and satisfaction to its owner comes gradually, because it is a child born of knowledge and persistent purpose.

"To earn wealth is nothing more than a slight burden upon the thoughtful man. Bearing that small burden consistently, month after month, year after year, accomplishes the final purpose.

"The five laws of gold offer a rich reward to the man who observes them. Each law is rich with meaning. Study them well. Learn them by heart. Live them each day and you will see their value, and they will enrich your life."

CHAPTER TEN

The Clay Tablets from Babylon

Professor Loyn Marvel
Oklahoma State University
Stillwater, OK 74074

Dear Professor Marvel,

The five clay tablets from your recent Babylon ruins excavation arrived with your letter. I found them fascinating and have spent many wonderful hours translating them. My goal was to complete all the translations before I answered.

The tablets arrived without damage, thanks to your careful packing. You will be excited, as we were, at the story they share. We expected some grand adventure, like the Arabian Nights. Instead, the tablets share the problems of a man named Dabasir and paying off his debts. It is amazing how so little has changed in five thousand years.

It's odd, but I found his story rather disconcerting. It struck a personal chord with me—so much wisdom I'd never heard before,

..ousand years ago, about a guy who got out of debt and started becoming wealthy. It's an intriguing thought. I wonder if his strategy would work as well today as it did in old Babylon. Effie and I are planning to try it out on our finances, which could be improved.

I wish you the best of luck with your worthy undertaking, and I look forward to helping you again.

Yours Sincerely,

Lee Thurman
Department of Middle Eastern Languages & Cultures
University of California, Berkeley
Berkeley, CA 94720

TABLET I

Now, when the moon becomes full, I, Dabasir, who has recently returned from slavery in Syria, am determined to pay my many debts and become a man of means, worthy of respect in my native city of Babylon. I hereby engrave upon the clay a permanent record of my affairs to guide and assist me in carrying out my greatest desires.

Under the wise advice of my good friend Mathon, the gold lender, I am determined to follow a precise plan that he says will lead any honorable man out of debt into means and self-respect.

This plan includes three purposes, which are my hope and desire.

First, the plan provides for my future prosperity.

To accomplish this, I will set aside and keep one-tenth of all I earn, for Mathon speaks wisely when he says:

"The man who keeps in his purse both gold and silver that he does not need to spend is in a position to help himself and his family and to be loyal to his king, for his heart is filled with self-respect.

"The man who has only a few coppers in his purse is indifferent to his family and to his king.

"But the man who has nothing in his purse is unkind to his family and disloyal to his king, for his own heart is bitter.

"Therefore, the man who wishes to prosper must have gold and silver coins jingling in his purse, so he can have in his heart love for his family and loyalty to his king."

Second, the plan provides I shall support and clothe my good wife, Sarratu, who has, with loyalty, returned to me from the house of her father. For Mathon says that if a man takes good care of a faithful wife, it will put self-respect into his heart and add strength and determination to his purposes.

Therefore, seven-tenths of all I earn shall be used to provide a home, clothes to wear, and food to eat, with a bit extra to spend, so our lives will not be lacking in pleasure and enjoyment. But Mathon bids us to take great care that we spend no more than seven-tenths of what I earn for these worthy purposes. Herein lies the success of the plan. I must live on this portion of my earnings and never use more, nor buy what I cannot pay for out of this portion.

TABLET II

Third, the plan provides that I will pay my debts out of my earnings.

Each time the moon is full, I will honorably and fairly divide two-tenths of my earnings among those who have trusted me and to whom I am indebted. Thus in due time all my debts will be paid.

Therefore, I list here every man's name to whom I am indebted and the honest amount of my debt.

- Fahru, the cloth weaver, 2 silver, 6 copper.
- Sinijar, the couch maker, 1 silver.
- Ahmar, my friend, 3 silver, 1 copper.
- Zankar, my friend, 4 silver, 7 copper.
- Askanir, my friend, 1 silver, 3 copper.
- Harinsir, the jewel maker, 6 silver, 2 copper.
- Diarbeker, my father's friend, 4 silver, 1 copper.
- Alkahad, the house owner, 14 silver.
- Mathon, the gold lender, 9 silver.
- Birejik, the farmer, 1 silver, 7 copper.

(From here on, the tablet is disintegrated and cannot be deciphered.)

TABLET III

To these creditors I owe a total of 119 pieces of silver and 141 pieces of copper. Because I owed these sums and saw no way to repay, in my folly I permitted my wife, Sarratu, to return to her father, and I left my native city to seek easy wealth elsewhere, only to find disaster and to see myself sold into the degradation of slavery.

Now that Mathon has shown me how I can repay my debts in small sums out of my earnings, I realize the great extent of my folly in running away from the results of my extravagances.

Therefore I have visited my creditors and explained to them that I have no resources with which to pay except my ability to earn, and that I intend to apply two-tenths of all I earn to my indebtedness, evenly and honestly. This much I can pay, but no more. If they are able to be patient, in time I will pay my obligations in full.

Ahmar, who I thought was my best friend, berated me bitterly, and I left him in humiliation. Birejik, the farmer, pleaded that I pay him first because he badly needs it. Alkahad, the house-owner, was angry and insisted he would make trouble for me unless I immediately paid him in full.

All the rest willingly accepted my proposal. I am now more determined than ever to carry it through, as I am convinced that it is easier to pay one's just debts than to avoid them. Even though I cannot meet the needs and demands of a few of my creditors, I will deal impartially with all of them.

TABLET IV

Again the moon shines full. I have worked hard with a free mind. Sarratu has supported my intentions to pay my creditors. Because of our wise determination, during the past moon I have earned the sum of nineteen pieces of silver. I did so by buying, for Nebatur, camels of sound wind and good legs.

I have divided this sum according to the plan. I have set aside one-tenth to keep as my own, and I have divided seven-tenths with my wife to pay for our living expenses. I divided two-tenths among my creditors as evenly as could be done in coppers.

I did not see Ahmar, but left his payment with his wife. Birejik was so pleased he wanted to kiss my hand. Old Alkahad alone was grouchy and said I must pay faster, to which I replied that if I am permitted to be fed and not worried, that alone would enable me to pay faster. All the others thanked me and spoke well of my efforts.

Therefore, at the end of one moon, I reduced my indebtedness by almost four pieces of silver and I possess almost two pieces of silver besides, to which no man has claim. My heart is lighter than it has been for a long time.

ЖК

Again the moon shines full. I have worked hard but with poor success. I have been able to buy only a few camels, and have earned a mere eleven silver pieces. Nevertheless, Sarratu and I have stood by the plan even though we have bought no new clothing and eaten little but the simplest of vegetables and herbs. Again I paid ourselves one-tenth of the eleven pieces, while we lived upon seven-tenths. I was surprised when Ahmar commended my payment, even though it was small. So did Birejik. Alkahad flew into a rage, but when I suggested he give back his portion if he did not want it, he became reconciled. The others were contented, as before.

Ж

Again the moon shines full, and I rejoice. I came upon a fine herd of camels and bought many sound ones, therefore my earnings were forty-two pieces of silver. This moon my wife and I have bought much needed sandals and clothing. Also, we have dined well on meat, luscious fruit, and the finest vegetables.

We have paid more than eight pieces of silver to our creditors. Even Alkahad did not protest.

Great is the plan, for it leads us out of debt and gives us wealth that is ours to keep.

Three times the moon has been full since I first carved upon this clay. Each time, I paid to myself one-tenth of all I earned. Each time, my wonderful wife and I have lived upon seven-tenths, even though it was sometimes difficult. Each time, I have paid two-tenths to my creditors.

In my purse I now have twenty-one pieces of silver that are mine, more than I ever owned before this day. It makes me hold my head up high, straighten my shoulders, and feel proud to walk among my friends.

Sarratu keeps our home well, and is well and attractively dressed. We are happy to be sharing this life together.

The plan is of untold value. It has made an honorable man of an ex-slave.

TABLET V

Again the moon shines full, and I remember that it is a long time since I carved a clay tablet. Twelve moons have come and gone. But this day I will not neglect my record, because upon this day I have paid the last of my debts. This is the day on which Sarratu and I celebrate thankfully and with great feasting that our greatest desires have been achieved.

Many things occurred on my last visit to my creditors that I will long remember. Ahmar begged my forgiveness for his unkind words and said I was the one of all others that he desired most for a friend.

Old Alkahad is not so bad after all, for he said, "You were once a piece of soft clay to be pressed and molded by any hand that touched you. But now you are a piece of bronze capable of holding an edge. If you need silver or gold at any time, come to me."

Nor is he the only one who holds me in high regard. Many others speak respectfully to me. Good Sarratu looks at me with a light in her eyes that makes a man have confidence in himself. I will never let her down again.

Yet it is the plan that has made my success. It has enabled me to pay all my debts and to have both gold and silver in my purse. I do recommend it to all who wish to get ahead. For truly, if it will enable an ex-slave to pay his debts and have gold in his purse, will it not help any man to find independence? Nor am I, myself, finished with it, for I am convinced if I follow it further, it will make me rich among men.

Professor Loyn Marvel
Oklahoma State University
Stillwater, OK 74074

Dear Professor Marvel,

If you come upon the ghost of Dabasir, that Babylonian camel trader, please do me a favor. Tell him his scribblings on these clay tablets have earned him a lifetime of gratitude from me and some university folks here in Berkeley.

You may recall that in my letter to you a year ago, I indicated that my wife, Effie, and I might try the old fellow's plan for getting out of debt and moving toward financial independence. For years we had been struggling, and getting deeper and deeper into debt. We paid everything we could out of our income, but barely broke even. We shopped at places that would give us credit, but paid much higher prices for the privilege. Our debt snowballed. In fact, for years I had been terrified that my growing debt load and plummeting credit rating might get me fired.

It developed into a downward spiral with no end in sight. We couldn't move to a less costly place because of how much we owed our current landlord. Even if we could pay him, we'd never pass a credit check on a new place. I felt there was no way out.

Then along came those tablets from that camel trader, with his description of his plan. His story motivated us to follow his system. What did we have to lose?

The first thing we did was open a special savings account, and set up an automatic transfer of 10% of our paychecks directly into that account. The idea of being able to set aside money for ourselves each month was quite motivating. It was a relief to think that soon we'd have some extra cash on hand for emergencies, rather than just hoping for the best and using credit cards when something goes wrong.

Next, we made a list, swallowed our pride, and contacted everyone we owed. I explained it was impossible for me to repay them on the schedule they had devised. I told them the only way I could repay them would be to use 20% of my income to pay them back, along with my other creditors. I showed each one exactly how much of that 20% would go toward their account each month. I also told them that until my debt was paid in full, our transactions would be on a cash-only basis.

They were quite reasonable. Our grocer, a wise old man, cut to the heart of the matter when he said, "That's fine with me. You haven't paid anything on your account in three years. If you pay for all you buy and then even a small amount on what you owe, that will be a big improvement." We made that case to our other creditors, and it helped them come around as well.

Finally, I had all of them sign an agreement saying they would not come after me as long as I paid as promised.

My wife and I then began planning how we were going to live on the 70% that would be left after we put 10% in savings and 20% toward debt. It was like an adventure to find ways make it work. I never would have expected it, but we actually enjoyed figuring out a way to live comfortably on that 70%. We started by dropping our cable TV service and switched to getting service from an antenna—for free! That gave us huge savings every month, and it inspired us to do more. We started bringing lunch to work instead of going out, and I realized I didn't need that double latte every day. Soon we just changed the way we thought about every expense, and asked ourselves, "Do we really need it?" We even looked at our food purchases and found that some of our favorite brands were simply not a good value.

To make a long story short, it did not prove to be as difficult as we thought it would be. We worked the plan cheerfully. It was like a load off my back to be getting our affairs in order and to no longer feel the pressure of past-due accounts.

I do need to share something with you about the 10% we set aside before paying everyone else. We were amazed at how quickly those monthly transfers added up. Before we knew it, we'd accumulated an amount equal to six months of our income—what a great feeling! We knew that would take care of most emergencies we might face, so we started to put that 10% into some sensible investments. We soon found that there is more pleasure in seeing our money grow than in spending it. We also found a way to reduce our tax liability, which gave us more cash flow for our plan—a spiral of a different nature.

It's an incredible feeling to know our savings are growing. When my teaching days are over, we should have enough to support us throughout our retirement years.

All of this is coming out of the same old paycheck. It's hard to believe, but true. All our debts are being paid down while our investments are increasing. And Effie and I seem to be getting along even better than before. How can this be? Who would believe there could be such a difference just from choosing to adopt a sound financial plan?

At the end of this year, all our debts will be paid. We will have even more to put into our investment account, and we'll be able to do some of the traveling we've yearned to do. Even so, we are determined to never again spend more than 70% of our income.

You can understand why we would like to extend our personal thank you to that old Babylonian camel trader. He saved us from the misery of never-ending debt. He must have been a good man with a good heart. He wanted others to benefit from his pain. I can only assume that was why he spent what must have been hours, over the course of that year, carving that clay.

He had a great deal of wisdom to share with those of us in debt and struggling to keep our heads above water, a message so important that after five thousand years it has risen out of the ruins of Babylon. Dabasir's message is just as valuable now as it was then.

Yours sincerely,

Lee Thurman
Department of Middle Eastern Languages & Cultures
University of California, Berkeley
Berkeley, CA 94720

EPILOGUE

[*Editor's note: In 1937, George S. Clason published* Gold Ahead: A Saga for Practical Treasure Hunters, *a book that included most of the stories from* The Richest Man in Babylon *as well as additional writings by E. McPherson Cole. Little is known about Cole, but he appears to have been an editor or collaborator for the 1937 publication. The following is the "Conclusion" from* Gold Ahead, *in which E. McPherson Cole introduces an excerpt from a monologue delivered by Clason. The monologue is valuable as one of few records we have of Clason stepping away from the wise men of Babylon and speaking directly to his readers.*]

Today, just as it was in the time of ancient Babylon, for those who manage money well, the rewards are many. For those who do not, the penalties are a shortage of money, financial embarrassment, debt, and needless heartache. This book shares knowledge of the correct principles for acquiring and handling money. My purpose in this conclusion is to show how anyone can use these principles to promote their own financial well-being.

Any person who is going to manage money successfully must be a financial manager, whether his accounts and operations are large or small. It applies to those with funds they can easily invest safely and profitably. It also applies to those who wish their earnings or incomes were sufficient to do more than barely make ends meet. It even applies to every member of a family who is dependent upon one or more earners for support. Managing a family's finances is a joint affair in which the needs of each member can best be taken care of by wisely adjusting the requirements of all.

In the system of "The Richest Man in Babylon," time is an important component of success. Given enough time, relatively small financial operations can grow to much larger dimensions. To Arkad, his future was not a hazy land where he hoped dreams would come true. It was a real land where time could be his ally, and where there would be stores of gold if one planned for them and worked to make his plans become realities.

Among Mr. Clason's writings, I discovered one in which this view of a tangible future is so impressively presented that I wish to quote from it here. The following is taken from his monograph entitled, "Choose the Road Where the Money Trees Grow." Here's what he said:

> Ahead, with the fascinating uncertainty of an unknown land, lies your future. *Waste no idle regrets on a past that is gone.* Look beyond the difficulties and problems of the present. The future is yours, and in it you are justified in expecting the realization of your most cherished desires.
>
> The ability to look ahead at a substantial distance into your future, and to see events that are waiting to occur, may seem unusual to say the least. So it is. And yet, this is what I feel I was permitted to do, and subsequent events have supported me in accepting that it actually happened. Certain things that I was permitted to see have come to pass exactly as I foresaw them. For others that are further into the future, I am looking forward to them with full confidence that they will also come to pass.

My most unusual experience occurred in a dream. I dreamt that I was standing in the center of a broad, clay-colored road out in the country. I could see it for a long way as it curved and twisted through a rolling, hilly district. As I looked, I gradually became aware that this road represented my life. Back as far as I could see, at the most distant point, was my early childhood. The point where I was standing was the present. Each bit of scenery in between was symbolic of one of the more important happenings of my life, and each turned into an animated picture of the event as my eyes rested upon it. Together they provided a vivid portrayal of the sequence of assorted experiences that join together to make one's life story.

As I stood there, a thought came with startling force: How wonderful it would be if I could turn around and look ahead into my future as clearly as I was looking back into my past. With a sudden resolve, I turned and looked in the opposite direction. Sure enough, the road—my road—continued on, far into the distant hills and valleys of my future years.

My first impression of what I saw was disappointing...or perhaps I should say surprising. I, like most folks, expect the future to be quite different from the past and the present. Yet I could see no difference. It was the same identical road continuing ahead with little change. A few paces forward or backward did not matter. It was the same sort of road that I had been following all my life.

Gradually the scenes ahead began to shape themselves into readable symbols, similar to the ones behind. With a strange feeling of awe I realized that, apparently, I was seeing unborn events, events destined to happen to me as I traveled this road ahead. Somehow I realized the vision would be fleeting, and I strained to see and interpret as much as I could. Reluctantly I was pulled back to consciousness. Because of my great desire to remember what I had seen, I impressed the pictures vividly upon my mind.

Naturally the question arises, did the future events I saw in my dream come to pass?

I can answer truly and without reservation, yes, many of those visions have come to pass and joined the bits of scenery along that portion of my road that lies in my past. Something like fifteen years have passed since it was my privilege to look into the future. I have traveled a long way along that road, and there is no question but that it is the same road I saw in my dream.

Since all who read this, whether you realize it or not, are following a road that, like mine, leads into a future where you wish desirable things to happen, I am going to tell you some confidential information about the events along my road, things I have learned after following it for so long.

When I first looked ahead and foresaw so many events depicted as major happenings in my future, I was somewhat skeptical. I hardly knew whether to accept them with a fatalistic philosophy—to take it for granted that some providence, divine or otherwise, ruled my destiny and had ordained these things to come to pass—or whether to take the matter-of-fact viewpoint and wave it all away as just a dream. However, it was not to be forgotten, especially when, as the years rolled by, these prophesied events began to happen.

Naturally, I became almost fatalistic, and thought it must be destiny after all. Those events that I most desired to happen were coming true. But as the years passed, I noticed that some that I preferred not to happen did not. Gradually it dawned upon me that, through my own desires supported by a definite determination, I could do much to help bring about those things I desired to happen—and, even more definitely, I could prevent the undesirable from coming to pass.

My original picture proved to be malleable, subject to alterations and changes of my own making. Nevertheless, my road ahead is just as real and just as tangible as it always was. I realize I have been most fortunate to have a definite road to follow. It has led me to the fulfillment of many cherished desires. It still guides me forward. I do not wander into the future without a purpose beyond just to keep moving. Along my road are other unborn events that I deeply wish to experience. Because I know my own ability to assist them in coming to pass, I look forward with confidence to their becoming realities in due time.

Your future stretches out ahead of you like a road leading into the distance. Along this road are unborn events, desires you wish to gratify, ambitions you wish to fulfill. Realize your ability to aid them in coming to pass. Look forward with confidence that they will become realities. Be the master of this future of yours, not its slave. You can, if you wish it to be so, make of it the kind of road you wish to follow.

That is Mr. Clason's vision of the future, and I like it. It is not a fantasy land of unrealistic events, but a real place where we will be liberally rewarded for our consistent efforts to prepare for our journey there. One area in which we will be particularly rewarded in the future is our ability to acquire and manage money.

The management of money is not an exact science like chemistry or mathematics. Neither is it a semi-exact science like spelling or grammar. Personal feelings and prejudices, family relationships, associations with others outside the family, all play an important part in the way we handle our incomes and our expenditures. For each of us, whether we have a great deal of money or only a little, the management of our resources is a constant and ever-changing problem.

The characters in this book were also confronted with financial problems—problems in getting money, in paying debts, in building up money reserves, and, even more important, problems in keeping the money they had acquired. If they met their problems wisely, they prospered; if not, they lost what they had, or failed to make what they might have made.

As the richest man in Babylon said to his friends,

> Recall that our wise teachers taught us there are two kinds of learning: one in which we learn things and know them, and another in which we learn how to find out about things we do not know.

The Babylon tales are a tremendous storehouse of financial knowledge and understanding, in which we can find much we will need to know. An official of a large bank went so far as to pronounce them a textbook for bankers. I would not limit their wisdom to the use of bankers. They are a textbook on the wise management of money in which can be found sane advice that applies, in general, to every kind of financial problem and, specifically, to a surprising number of problems that any of us may be called upon to address. They supply a reference book to which we can turn and find wise advice regarding the problems that confront us personally. They will help us arrive at wise decisions in matters where an unwise decision would cause heavy loss and long, bitter regrets.

Money that comes into our possession is our stepping stone to securing larger amounts. Therefore, it is just as important to know how to keep money as it is to be able to make it. The possession of a sum of money puts us in the position of being a financial manager—a manager of money. If we lose it or let it get away, with it goes the opportunity to use it to make more money.

These Babylon tales are a practical course of instruction in the management of money. One must not be misled by their simplicity and overlook their wisdom. They contain truths that every one of us can apply successfully to our own financial advancement. Some of these truths are self-evident, even to the casual reader. Others cannot be fully appreciated until we have an opportunity to use them or see how precisely they will apply to our own problems or those of others in our midst.

By repeated reading of this book, one learns to look at all problems related to their personal financial advancement through the eyes of the wise men of old Babylon. One learns to reason out the logical results of financial transactions. Money management thus ceases to be a series of experiments based on impractical hopes or influenced by unsound sentiments. Instead, it becomes a carefully planned program that will avoid the usual pitfalls that are always waiting to separate the unwary from their money.

To those who will turn to these pages to learn the things they need to know in order to act wisely, the Babylon tales are a goldmine of wise advice and suggestions. The wisdom of these wise, rich men is at the disposal of all who come to them for help. They are waiting, through these pages, to act as your instructors and confidential advisors.

STUDY GUIDE

FOR FINANCIAL INDEPENDENCE

Who can become financially independent?

Who are the "fortunate few" who can escape the drudgery of living paycheck to paycheck, and enjoy all the benefits of financial independence?

Are they the tight wads, the penny pinchers?

Or are they just the lucky ones?

None of these is an accurate characterization—at most, they apply only to a small minority of financially successful people. Financial independence is not limited to tightwads, penny pinchers, or those who just happen to benefit from the luck of the draw. It is within the reach of every person who has a burning desire to achieve it, to the degree that he or she is determined to study and to work toward it, in spite of the obstacles that will inevitably arise along the way. Financial success is the logical result of consistent effort in the right direction.

How do you know what the right direction is for attaining your financial goals? Jim Rohn, one of my favorite authors, has said, "Whatever you want, study it. If you want to be happy, study happiness. If you want to be wealthy, study wealth."

I couldn't agree more.

What do you want? Whatever it is, you can find ways to study it. There are books available today on almost every topic—you can find them online, in stores, and in libraries. There are YouTube videos galore. And of course, you can Google any topic and find a treasure trove of information. You have every opportunity to find the resources you need to study anything you want to achieve.

This Study Guide, along with the stories throughout this book about the wealthy men of ancient Babylon, are an excellent way to begin your study of how to become financially independent. If you make a commitment to yourself to make learning a lifelong habit, you'll be well on your way to achieving all the things that matter most to you—including financial success. Know what you want, and study it.

There are five lessons in this Study Guide. Inside each lesson are questions for you to ponder. Some of them are fairly simple and straightforward, while others invite you to take a closer look at your own values, habits, and the choices you want to make in your life. Spending time with all the questions will help you absorb the teachings offered by Clason's characters so you'll remember them for life.

Study Plan

1. Purchase a journal or another type of notebook that you can use to record your work on this Study Guide. You'll use it to write out questions and answers, make lists and notes, and any other thoughts or observations that come along. Be sure to date every entry you make.

   Each lesson includes a list of questions for you to answer. You'll use your journal to write your answers, of course, but I recommend you also write out the questions. It might seem an unnecessary burden, but doing so reinforces the question in your mind, and may enhance your understanding. It has the added benefit of eliminating the need to refer back to the book each time you want to take a fresh look at the question you're answering.

   I also recommend you use a page in your journal to create a net worth statement. This is simply a list of what you own (your "assets"), and a list of what you owe (your "liabilities"). When you take what you own and subtract what you owe, you arrive at your net worth. It's a good idea to do this once a year to see your progress. It's common to feel like you're standing still, when in fact you are moving closer to your goal—it just may not feel like it in when you're in the midst of your daily grind. Tracking your net worth from one year to the next will help you realize just how far you've come—a positive reinforcement of your hard work and discipline. (Just to share how this can become a source of joy, in my first net worth statement I included the value of my clothes to try to make my net worth a positive number. I didn't make it. As I worked up a new statement each year, I was able to enjoy seeing my progress, and it helped me stay the course—especially in the times when that felt difficult.)

Starting this journal now and adding to it in the years to come will provide a fascinating record of your financial journey, and the personal growth that is likely to occur along the way. Years from now, I'm confident you'll be able to look through the pages and see just how far you've come and how much your thoughts have changed.

2. Begin with Lesson 1 as the foundation of the Study Guide. It's designed to help fire up your motivation to complete the remaining lessons—but also to create inspiration for you to implement the things you'll learn from them as you build stability and success in your financial life. (For your work on Lesson 1, skip Steps 3 and 5 in this Study Plan, and any other instruction to refer back to the stories in this book.)
3. As you work your way through Lessons 2 through 5, begin by reading the chapter the lesson is drawn from. Even if you've read the chapter before, read it again as you begin this deeper study.
4. Next, read through the lesson—but don't answer the questions just yet. Find a time when you can read it carefully, when you

won't be hurried or interrupted. Take a day or two to do some thinking about the observations at the beginning of the lesson and the questions it asks. Let your mind turn it all over for a while and see what new insights emerge.

5. Now, spend some time on a detailed study of the chapter the lesson is based on. Read through the chapter every day for five days, to allow the teaching to be indelibly inscribed in your mind. Your goal is to know those teachings so well that they become a permanent and practical part of your knowledge base.
6. It's now time to focus on the lesson itself. To get the maximum value from it, as you work through each question, write it down in your journal. Then find the passage in the story that the question refers to, and copy that down along with the page number where you find it. Then write out your answer to the question using all the examples and logic at your command. Taking your time to go through these steps will help you internalize and understand the material—and the better you know the material, the better it will serve you later. Finally, remember to write down the date when you do this work.
7. Move on to the next lesson and repeat the process outlined above.

The five lessons in this Study Guide go right to the heart of the basic theme of The Richest Man in Babylon—that anyone with the ability to earn income who has a burning desire to become financially independent can do so. The lessons focus on the following topics:

Lesson 1. Find Your Inspiration

Lesson 2. Chapter Seven: The Richest Man in Babylon

Lesson 3. Chapter Eight: Seven Cures for a Lean Purse

Lesson 4. Chapter Nine: The Five Laws of Gold

Lesson 5. Chapter Ten: The Clay Tablets of Babylon

To be clear, all chapters in The Richest Man in Babylon are worthy of study, and I urge you to study every one of them in detail. For the purpose of your in-depth work in this Study Guide, I chose the four chapters that I feel will impact your life the most. The addition of the all-important Lesson 1, "Find Your Inspiration," will provide a foundation to carry you through these pages and your continued commitment to your financial future.

Lesson I
Find Your Inspiration

For most people, financial success does not come easily. It's the result of hard work, applying discipline every day and for years on end to implement a sound plan, and a willingness to do whatever it takes to overcome obstacles. That kind of sustained effort can be difficult to maintain. This lesson is designed to set you up for success by helping you figure out what makes it worth all that effort—for you. Everyone has different goals they find worth working for, and different values that will make becoming wealthy a meaningful achievement. The things that motivated me to put in that sustained effort are different from those that will motivate you.

As you work through the questions in this lesson, you'll discover what it will take to keep you going throughout the coming years—or decades—until you reach your financial goals.

Start with Why

I wish I could tell you that sticking to your plan for becoming wealthy will always be easy. It won't be. There will be times when you want to toss your spending plan out the window and buy that special something that you're sure will bring you lots of joy—or at least a nice bit of short-term happiness. There will be other times when you're tempted to get in on some get-rich-quick idea your buddy is excited about, even though you know the great teachers in The Richest Man in Babylon would call it a huge mistake. Building wealth takes time, and there are countless temptations and obstacles that will threaten to derail your plan and cost you buckets of money.

So how will you stay on track?

Motivation. Keep your eye on the prize. Reach for the stars. Sounds good, but it only works if the star you're reaching for is one that genuinely lights you up. But don't worry—you're about to identify what prizes or stars or dreams matter enough to you to make all the effort worthwhile.

A great way to help you stay on track is to "start with why." Why do you want to be financially successful? That is, what desires and dreams do you have that are only possible if you achieve your goal of financial independence? Does your "why" inspire you? To overcome the challenges you will inevitably face, your "why" must be a strong one. If it is, it will help you sustain your commitment to be disciplined about managing your finances. And when obstacles present themselves (we'll take a closer look at that on page 13, "Be Prepared to Overcome Obstacles"), your "why" will help you figure out the "how," so that each time you encounter a new roadblock you'll simply alter your course to arrive safely at your destination.

The following is a list of questions and exercises designed to illuminate your values, to help you become more consciously aware of what matters most to you in this life...deep down. Your underlying values influence your decisions and actions in ways that move you toward your preferred future, the one you'll arrive at when you've lived your best life. This process of drawing out your values and bringing them into the light of day makes them even more powerful, and can have a deep and long-lasting impact on your life. We're using it here to help you attain financial independence, but you can also use it to help you reach other goals—a healthier lifestyle, the right relationship, a career you love, or anything else that's worth working toward.

Let's get started.

1. What gets you out of bed in the morning? What keeps you up at night? The first answer is your "carrot"—your reward. The second is your stick—usually an effective deterrent. Most of us need both a carrot and a stick. Personally, I prefer carrots. But knowing the things that drive you emotionally can be a major motivator toward your preferred future, the one you want most to create for yourself. How can you use your personal carrots and sticks to help you achieve your financial goals?

2. How do you want to be remembered? With this question you might say we're starting with the end. At the end of your life, how do you want people to remember you? Or here's another way to look at it: What would you like them to say about you at your 85th birthday party? How would improving your financial condition help you get there? What changes do you need to make to realize those improvements?

3. Who do you want to be? Be proud of the future You. The future You should inspire you. Describe the future You.

4. This part will take a little time, but it's well worth it—the first time I did it, it was truly life changing. With your answers to the previous three questions in mind, answer this one: "What's important—to me—about financial independence?" The "to me" part is key. We're not looking for what you think you should answer, or what the world says, but what is important to you? Now ask that question at least four more times, and come up with different answers. To help you get started, here are a few examples:

    a. I can travel.
    b. I can be free to choose what I want to do.
    c. I can buy the stuff I want.
    d. I can quit my job.
    e. I can give to charity and make a meaningful difference.

Now, looking over your list, which of the items on it is most important...to you?

Next, ask yourself, "Is there anything more important to me about being financially independent, that's not already on the list?" If so, what is it? Write it down, and look over your list again. Anything else to add here?

For me, the most important thing on the list was freedom to choose what I want to do. I value freedom highly.

Now we come to the conclusion of this exercise. We've narrowed down the "what." But why is this important to you? For me, the "what" is financial freedom. Why is financial freedom important to me? It allows me to do the things I want to do. If I continue to work, it's because I want to, not because I have to. Financial freedom allows me to make quality choices for my family, myself, and charities I care about. It gives me options—for education, health care, vacations, philanthropy, and more. That freedom to choose is what drives me. That may or may not be your why, but defining yours will help you achieve your goals.

Identify Your Dreams and Desires

Having money—and especially wanting to have money—sometimes gets a bad rap. Since money allows you to buy material goods, it's sometimes viewed as a lesser goal than, say, wanting to be a better person, or a desire to make a contribution to society.

But here's the thing. Those values are not mutually exclusive. Many very wealthy people are also very good people. And it's not difficult to find examples of how wealth can allow you to make an enormous contribution to making life better for others. Goals like that are perfectly good reasons to strive for financial success. They may even be so important to you that they're all you need to inspire you to do the work it takes to acquire great wealth.

Still, that doesn't mean you have to—or that you should—forego things that make your own life better. Material things, even. A nicer house, an amazing sound system for your very cool backyard patio, the ability to take your family on trips to exotic places...all those things and whatever else makes it onto your wish list are perfectly legitimate desires. Knowing what makes financial success worth having—for you—is what will give you the motivation to keep going when your discipline falters or obstacles present themselves.

In this section we'll work on identifying the dreams and desires that matter to you. Your list will be different from anyone else's, and that's as it should be. Spend the time here to dream about what your life could be like if you had a little more money...or a lot.

Have fun with this. What better way to brighten up an afternoon or three than thinking about what you'd most like to spend money on when—not if—you have it.

Here we go.

1. Make a list of things you'd like to have—not just items, but experiences as well, and even changes you'd like to make in your lifestyle. Include the small things, like maybe a short day trip or that cool new gizmo your friend told you about. If you need a new car, or would just like a nicer one with the latest bells and whistles, write that down, too. What are some things you've always wanted to do, but can't afford yet? Whether it's a vacation, more frequent trips to visit relatives, or a night out at the theater every month, it goes on the list. Do you want a bigger house, or would you like to move to an exotic coastal area...or buy a boat and sail around the world? Yep, include that, too. Make this a list of your dreams—the ones you can achieve fairly

easily and those that will take more time and effort, but also the ones that seem like crazy fantasies, because...well, they might not be so crazy after all. Best of all, putting them all on the list is a great way to motivate yourself to put Arkad's Seven Cures for a Lean Purse to work for you.

2. Next, make a chart with three columns. Label the first column "Easy," the second column "Challenging," and the third "Audacious." (Yes—you're allowed to identify some big, wonderful, audacious dreams to aim for.) The first list, "Easy," will include those items that are easily within your ability and resources to obtain if you decide to go after them. The second list, "Challenging," will contain those items that call for more money, time, or effort than those in the "Easy" column. Obtaining them is feasible, but it will be much more challenging. The dreams you place in the last column, "Audacious," will be flat-out tough to achieve—in fact, as you imagine them now they may seem downright impossible, mere fantasies. But they're things that get your heart racing a bit. They're big and exciting! And that's the point—that rush of energy you feel when you think about them will inspire you to stick to your plan and make your dreams—the small ones and the big ones—a reality.

3. Now place each item from your initial list into one of the three columns, "Easy," "Challenging," or "Audacious. This is an effective way to identify your desires and put them right in front

of your eyes for your consideration. It allows you to make conscious choices about which of your desires are worth spending your time and money on—and it helps you waste neither.

4. Your next step is to go through the list of items in your "Easy" column. Be deliberate, evaluate one at a time, and decide which ones you'd like to take steps now to attain. For the others, if you still want to attain them, write down when you believe you can realize that goal. When you review your journal in the months and years to come, you'll be fascinated to see how your timeline changed as you postponed some goals and met others sooner than you expected.

5. Next, consider the items in your "Challenging" column. Decide which ones would be most worth the effort required, and cross off any that don't seem to merit the necessary time, energy, and resources. You'll have a better chance of succeeding in realizing the goals that matter to you if you say no to those you don't really care about. For the items you say yes to, write down the year you'd like to enjoy them. Do any conflict with the timeline on your "Easy" list? If so, adjust both timelines until you feel you have a plan that's realistic. Get excited! There's real power in writing out these lists and including a date—it helps you move forward in achieving your goals. All that's left is to lay out your plans and start working for them.

6. For the items in the "Audacious" column—the things that may now seem impractical or impossible—look them over carefully. Spend some time thinking about each one, and notice what feeling it evokes in you. Do you feel a genuine desire to achieve it? Or is it just a sense that "it would be nice"? If it's the latter, cross if off your list. The items that remain should all be things that have strong pull for you, things that would bring you a great deal of joy or satisfaction. Now, write down a year next to those that remain. It's likely that the years in which you hope to achieve your "Audacious" goals will be farther out than those for your "Challenging" goals.

7. I understand that it can be tough to envision achieving goals that seem so far out of reach at this point in your life. But it's important, because with time, money, and focused effort, chances are you can achieve far, far more than you now imagine. It's much like looking at the horizon. From where you sit now, that's as far as you can see. But if you put one foot in front of the other, again and again and again, one day you arrive at that point that was once the limit of what you could see—and from that point, you can see much more. And so it is with financial progress.

8. This exercise should get your heart thumping. You've written down your desires, your dreams, and arranged them according to how challenging it will be to attain them. You now have a

vision of exciting things for your future! And as success coach Larry Wilson says, "The power of the vision pulls you there."

Be Prepared to Overcome Obstacles

Now that we know what your "why" is, and have identified the dreams and desires you'll fulfill when you build your financial future, you have all the inspiration and motivation you need to get started. But since we know there will inevitably be obstacles along the way—or, as I like to call them, challenges—let's look ahead to how you'll use that motivation to help you overcome those challenges. It's time to explore some strategies that will help you stay on track when the going gets tough.

It's impossible to anticipate all the challenges you'll face in the coming years. But there are a few areas where many people run into trouble. By taking a look at those now and identifying some strategies for overcoming them, you'll begin developing the skills to dig into the root of the problem and create a plan to resolve it. As you explore the things that seem now to stand between you and your goals, remember that success is sweetest when we've overcome obstacles in a practical, disciplined, and ethical way.

1. Begin by writing down the challenges that are currently slowing your progress toward financial success. Your list might include debt, a responsibility to support others, people who "keep me down," a lack of training or education, a perceived lack of opportunity to overcome challenges—anything you feel interferes with your ability to get ahead financially.

2. Spend some time focusing on each challenge on your list. What ideas come to mind that would help you overcome it? Write them down. Be brutally frank here. The solutions might seem obvious, but writing them down makes them real—and more achievable. For example, you might decide to avoid spending time around people who hold you back by undermining your confidence. You could go back to school, or break a habit that undermines your health. Or you can create a plan to spend more time working on what's most important to you rather than on things you don't really care about.

3. Can you think of someone you admire, a role model, who has been in your shoes and overcome a challenge similar to yours? When you find yourself in a tough situation, ask, "What would my role model do?" Develop a network of people who have demonstrated an ability to rise above tough situations. Napoleon Hill, in his brilliant, must-read-for-life book *Master-Key to Riches*, calls this your "mastermind group." It can include people you know personally as well as some you've only read about. Lean on them to help you respond to life's challenges in ways that help you move forward in a positive way. Getting angry in a conversation? Ask yourself what your model in this area would do. Thinking about putting an expensive item on your credit card? How would your model for smart spending handle that purchase? Whether you meet with a model for coffee once a month or just think of one of them when you have

a tough decision to make, let your mastermind group become your team of personal consultants.

4. Make a list of habits you can develop, starting today, that would help you overcome your challenges. Your list might include going to bed earlier, getting up earlier, eating better, not starting to do things that are time wasters, setting goals, reading great books, and so on.

5. Speaking of reading great books, *The 10 Natural Laws of Successful Time and Life Management: Proven Strategies for Increased Productivity and Inner Peace*, by Hyrum Smith, has been one of the most influential books in my life. Put it on your must-read reading list along with *The Master-Key to Riches.*

Lesson 2

Chapter Seven: "The Richest Man in Babylon"

In Lessons 2 through 5, we'll work directly with the material in a few of my favorite chapters from The Richest Man in Babylon. We'll begin here in Lesson 2 with Chapter Seven, and the story of how Arkad shared his understanding of money and wealth with his friends, who were still struggling to make ends meet.

One of the most important teachings Arkad offered deals with the first basic principle behind successful wealth accumulation: your right to keep a portion of what you earn. Even if you earn a large income, you can't accumulate wealth if you spend more than you make. A small income handled judiciously will, in the long run, provide much more satisfaction, enjoyment, and worldly possessions than a larger one handled poorly. Whether your income is large or small or something in between, it's essential to study how to handle your resources successfully and skillfully. Then, by applying sound strategies for using those resources to build more wealth, you can look forward to the benefits it can provide.

Questions

1. Explain in detail the two reasons Arkad gave for his friends' failure to acquire enough to eke out more than a bare existence, in spite of their hard and consistent work.

2. From your own experiences, think of an example (or a few examples) of someone coming into sudden wealth. Write a description of this example, and how it worked out. Did this person end up with permanent financial success or was the financial gain eventually lost? If you can't think of an example, do you agree with Arkad's opinion? Give your reasons.

3. As a youth, Arkad possessed the potential for financial success. As a result, he succeeded in becoming far wealthier than his friends. Should we infer, then, that his friends did not possess similar, if not equal, potential? Share your opinion about what qualities are essential to financial success.

4. As a youth, Arkad was determined to enjoy the better things in life. Explain the two prerequisites he considered most important.

5. What single rule did Algamish, the moneylender, give to Arkad as the first step on the road to wealth? Can you think of a better one? Give reasons.

6. After Arkad had begun his journey to becoming wealthy, how did Algamish advise him to build up his wealth, other than

increasing his earnings? In what ways can you apply our modern-day investment opportunities to his strategy?

7. To see how a little extra money saved now can make a big difference to you down the road, look up the value of $100 after 5 years, 10 years, and 25 years when it earns compounded interest. (Use different rates of return, such as 1%, 5%, 8%, and 10%, to see how important that is to your outcome.) To find a calculator to do that for you, go to www.Investor.gov, then type "compound interest calculator" in the search box. Explore what happens to a single investment of $100 over time, and also what happens if you add $100 every month.

8. At what point in the acquisition of money did Algamish advise Arkad to pay himself? Explain why this is the best time.

9. In this chapter, Arkad describes his first investment and explains how it turned out. Write out a similar fictitious experience for yourself in which you make an investment that turns out the same way. Select modern people and business conditions, but show how the logical conclusion would be similar.

10. Repeat the exercise in question #9, using Arkad's second investment as an example.

11. What was Arkad's next error? Describe a similar error someone might make in modern times, and explore how Algamish's advice would still be useful.

12. Explain the three great, fundamental lessons Arkad learned that were the basis of his further financial success.

13. Why did Arkad disagree with his friends when they said he was just lucky that Algamish had made him an heir?

14. Explain your thoughts on how important willpower is in achieving financial success, and why.

15. What plan would you recommend to those who must rely on their incomes to meet basic needs, and have a strong desire to become financially independent?

16. Was Arkad's advice to his friends to save 10% financially crippling? Do you believe an average person or family can decrease their living expenses by 10% without serious inconvenience? What are some things you could do now to decrease your living expenses by 10%?

17. Why did Algamish return again and again, over extended periods of time, to visit Arkad and offer him guidance? Was that important for Arkad's success?

18. In what ways did Arkad need to progress before further opportunities became available to him? Why was that important?

19. There was a turning point in Arkad's career when he made a definitive start toward his future success. At that point he ceased

merely making ends meet, because he had a vision to guide him. State when you think this occurred and why. Do you feel you have arrived at such a point in your career? Give your reasons. Remember, you're never too old to set new goals.

Lesson 3

Chapter Eight: "Seven Cures for a Lean Purse"

As we saw in Lesson 1, your journey to become financially independent starts with keeping a portion of your income for your future. If you make a million dollars a year but spend a million and one, you won't accumulate wealth.

Once you commit to saving a portion of every dollar you make, it's time to adopt a sound financial action plan—a strategy for managing your income, your spending, and how you'll put your growing savings to work for you. A good plan is the foundation of your success in building wealth. As they say, if you fail to plan, you simply plan to fail.

In this lesson we'll explore key elements of a plan of action for your personal financial affairs. The fundamentals shared in Chapter Eight, "The Seven Cures for a Lean Purse," will help you succeed not only with your finances, but in many other areas of your life as well. They can even be adapted to help you successfully operate a business.

As you answer the list of questions in this portion of the Study Guide, think of it as a way to begin building a practical plan for yourself—one that carries you forward to your preferred financial future.

Questions

1. Sargon, the king of Babylon, was facing a transitional time between a period of plenty and one of hardship for people in his kingdom, an ebb and flow experienced by societies throughout history. Can you identify parallel periods in modern times?

2. In recent times, many supposed "experts" and politicians have encouraged people to spend freely in order to help the economy. Do you believe your spending and saving habits should change based on the economy at large? Do you think when individuals practice healthy financial management it has any impact on the economy in general? Why or why not? Is your answer different regarding short-term versus long-term impact?

3. Did Arkad advise the men in his class to wait to start saving until after they increased their income? What were the reasons behind the advice he gave?

4. Arkad shared that, even when he "carried a lean purse and cursed it because there were not enough coins in it to satisfy [his] desires," he had little difficulty in getting along on 9/10 of his earnings. In fact, he told his students, "I managed to get along just as well as before. I was no less able to buy the things I needed." I suspect you'll have a similar experience—but you

won't know until you try. Write out a budget for yourself that has you getting along on 9/10 of your present expenditures.

5. In his teaching of The Second Cure, "Control Your Expenses," what observation did Arkad make about what happens to expenses when income goes up? List some reasons why you believe this is so often the case.
6. In what ways can you adapt Arkad's plan to eliminate unnecessary expenses in your own budget?
7. Do you consider a budget a useless bother, or do you agree with Arkad that it is an ally in defending your most cherished desires against less important demands? Give your reasons.
8. Define the difference between hoarding and building up a fortune. What do you think Arkad would have thought about this question?
9. Describe your views about wealth. Are they positive? If negative, could this be an obstacle preventing you from becoming wealthy?
10. Explain in detail the three factors Arkad recommends we consider when making an investment.
11. When making an investment, should you rely entirely on your own judgment, or should you seek the opinions of others? If you seek advice from others, who are the best candidates to provide it?

12. Do you—or would you—benefit from owning your own home? There are pros and cons to home ownership. Benefits might include the opportunity to build equity in your home, pride of ownership, and eventually owning your home without having to make mortgage payments. Among the downsides are having responsibility for all maintenance, being anchored geographically, and the likelihood of having more expenses than you would if you were renting. Make a list of pros and cons as they apply to your situation. Which choice could you make today that would lead to the best outcome for you twenty years from now? Why?

13. If you have a house payment, should you consider it a necessary living expense? Or is your payment effectively going into an investment? Or should it be divided between those two? Approximately how much of your payment goes to what you owe (your principal)? How much goes to interest? The allocation between principal and interest changes with every payment. To understand this better, look at your amortization schedule. (For help, visit www.Investopedia.com and search for "amortization schedule definition.") If you pay more than the minimum required payment on your mortgage, where does the additional amount go? (Hint: It doesn't go to interest.)

14. Arkad encourages his students to find ways to protect themselves against unexpected needs (like unemployment, sickness, death, disability) and from a reduction in income that often occurs

when one gets older. What opportunities do we now enjoy for financial protection that did not exist in Babylon? How much protection should you have? How much do you have?

15. State the methods Arkad used to increase his income when he was a scribe. How can you apply these methods to your own situation?

16. There is an old saying that tells us luck is what happens when opportunity meets preparedness. Do you believe that the person who prepares himself well is more likely find great opportunities? Can you cite an example of someone who progressed because he was ready when the right opportunity came along?

17. Review the four things that Arkad tells us "a man must do if he respects himself." Give your reasons for each.

18. In your own words, write out a summary of The Seven Cures. Post them in a conspicuous place where you'll see them and read them often. Make them a part of your daily thinking so they help your purse grow fatter and fatter.

LESSON 4

Chapter Nine: "The Five Laws of Gold"

Each of us is subject to many emotional influences and intellectual distractions that can influence our decisions and the actions that follow. This lesson will help you understand some of those factors, and the ways they can derail progress toward financial independence. It will also help you prepare to resist their influence as one of the many challenges you'll face on your journey.

As you'll discover, managing these challenges is not as difficult as it may seem, because the path to financial success is not a crooked, wandering trail—it's a precise, well-traveled route, as Nomasir and the other characters in the stories of this book illustrate. Even better, past travelers—like Nomasir and the authors of this book—are happy to advise like-minded people like you.

In Lesson 3 we'll explore The Five Laws of Gold, which beautifully crystalize the key principles that will help you to realize your financial goals. I urge you to memorize these laws. They will help you avoid negative influences and distractions so you can make wise choices as you take each step toward greater wealth. They also provide tools you can use to make sound judgements regarding the investments you'll make.

The path to wealth may not be an easy one. But with Nomasir's tale in Chapter Nine and The Five Laws of Gold he shares, your path will be easier and more certain. And it will be worth every bit of effort you give to it.

Questions

1. Nomasir left Babylon and went to a sister city, Nineveh, seeking opportunities. It is often said the grass is greener on the other side of the fence. Is it wise to seek an opportunity in a new location, or perhaps a different field of work or expertise? Or is it better to stay on familiar turf? Is there a handicap in being a stranger in a strange land? List the advantages and disadvantages of making such a change. List the advantages and disadvantages of staying where you are geographically and professionally.

2. Can you explain how the men in the caravan with the white horse collaborated with the wealthy man in Nineveh to cheat travelers? Do you see similarities in methods used by modern-day con men? Consider the common scam known as a Ponzi scheme, in which the schemer builds a pyramid of victims, taking money from more and more people to cover promises made to previous victims. Why are these scams so often successful at getting people to part with their money?

3. Can you think of an example of someone who bought a business, even though he or she had no prior training or experience running such a business? If so, describe how it worked out. If

you're not familiar with an actual case like that, what do you believe the probability of success would be?

4. Did Nomasir take a big chance going into business with someone he barely knew? Can you think of any examples in which a partnership like that succeeded?

   If you were to look for a partner to join you in a business venture, what skills, experience, or personality traits would you expect to yield a successful outcome? Should your partner be skillful in selling, accounting, marketing, manufacturing, management, or something else? What qualities do you think would indicate an individual would not be a good business partner for you?

   How do these factors rate, in terms of importance, relative to having a business partner you can trust?

5. Some save first, then spend what's left over. Others spend first, then invest what's left over. Is the choice of what comes first important? Which choice, in the long run, is most likely to lead to financial independence? Why?

6. The First Law of Gold tells us that "gold comes gladly" to someone who saves a portion of his income for his future. Can you give reasons why money comes more easily to those who have saved a part of their income than to those who haven't? Why do spenders have more financial distress than savers?

7. The Second Law of Gold teaches us to put our money to work, so it can make more money for us. Can you give reasons why

money appears to work hard for some, while others never manage to have their money generate much income? Do you think their thought processes are different? If so, how do they differ?

8. The Third Law tells us to invest "under the guidance of wise and trustworthy advisors." What qualifications do you think a wise advisor should have? What about a trustworthy one? If you're not sure, research the qualifications required to become a CERTIFIED FINANCIAL PLANNER™ (CFP®). The website at www.LetsMakeAPlan.org is a good place to start.

9. The idea that it takes money to make money may seem strange, but it has merit. Do you think this is always true? Can you name an example of someone who gradually built up substantial wealth without having a large income? (If you can't come up with someone, Google Earl Crawly, a parking lot attendant.)

10. The Fourth Law cautions us against investing in things we don't know much about, unless we do it under the guidance of a trustworthy, knowledgeable advisor. Name a time in your life when you lost money. Was the loss related to your knowledge—or lack thereof—of the entity you invested in? Was there any additional research you could have done, before you invested, that might have prevented the loss? What did you learn from the experience?

Have you ever used the advice of a financial professional who does not make money on the transaction, or who has no personal stake in your investment?

Look up the word fiduciary. Should a financial professional be a fiduciary?

Ultimately, who is responsible for your success in achieving financial independence?

11. The Fifth Law makes a strong statement warning us to avoid following the recommendations of "tricksters and schemers," or attempting to force our money to earn "impossible" returns. Describe an example or examples of a time when someone lost money—or, in Nomasir's terms, when money fled someone—when he tried investing in a "get-rich-quick" plan. Can you name an instance in which someone you know did well on such a plan? If so, how did it work out in the long run? Is there ever a time when it's okay to skip evaluating an investment's risk and return? It may sound painfully obvious, but repeat after me: "If it sounds too good to be true...." If you are presented with an "opportunity" you want to believe is true, but your inner voice is saying it sounds unrealistic, trust that inner voice.

12. What led to Nomasir's ability to free himself from the idea of getting rich quickly, and instead seek ways to put himself on more solid financial ground? Do you feel many people have to go through a similar shift in their thinking? If so, why do you

believe that's the case? What can you do to avoid this potentially expensive education yourself?

13. Would you consider the slave master's plan to buy enough bronze for the city gates a sound business proposition? State your reasons. Did he have a backup plan? If so, what was it?

14. State the advantages of a mastermind investment group like the one Nomasir joined. Make a list of wise, seasoned individuals whose ideas or work you can study—or perhaps even be part of a mastermind group you create yourself.

    Research the benefits of mutual funds. Here's a web page to get you started: Go to www.sec.gov/investor, then scroll down to "Publications" and click on "Mutual Funds – A Guide for Investors."

    In what ways do mutual funds offer advantages that are similar to having a mastermind advisory group? In what ways do they fall short?

15. Nomasir came to believe that financial wisdom is more valuable than gold. Do you agree with him? Why or why not?

    Which is more valuable, time or money? Why? Google Jim Rohn's opinion on this. Or go to YouTube and search for "Jim Rohn - Time is more valuable than money." Do you agree with him? Why or why not?

16. Kalabab states that he didn't gain wealth by using some strange magic, but by using sound financial practices instead. Why might some people, who really shouldn't, buy lottery tickets or

try to win big at gambling? What are their motivations? Do you know of anyone who has won big and found long-term financial independence as a result? Why is it important to focus on a logical, time-tested, and practical plan?

17. Have you lost money through an unwise decision or action? Does the decision haunt you? If so, write about the incident in detail. As you write, explore the reasons you chose to make the decision or take the action you did. (Don't be too hard on yourself—we've all done it!) Use the experience as a school, not an anchor.

18. Make a list of all investments you have made and loans you've taken that were unprofitable. For each one, write a brief statement describing why it was unprofitable. Next, do the same for your profitable investments and loans. What are the differences between those that were profitable and those that were not?

19. Nurturing your desire for wealth might seem like an exercise in self-indulgence, but it can actually help you achieve your financial goals. As Kalabab puts it, "In the strength of your own desires is a magic power." If you focus on your dream of attaining financial independence, how will it help you make careful decisions about your money, or lead more quickly to financial success?

20. As we discussed in Lesson 1, when your desire for financial success is strong, you'll be motivated to put in the effort it takes

to make your goals a reality. To take that a step further, when you begin to see the results of your efforts, it makes sense to reinforce them—it's just one more way to motivate yourself to stay disciplined and keep working to ensure your financial future.

What do you do—or could you do—to reinforce your efforts to become financially independent? (As an example, when you reach a certain financial goal, you might eat at a nice restaurant or treat yourself to some other nice indulgence you wouldn't normally spend money on.) What kind of reinforcement, or reward, is effective for you? Is it important to do this on a regular basis?

21. Memorize The Five Laws of Gold. Be able to repeat them in sequence and in random order. As your money grows, use these laws as a yardstick. Let them guide your decisions. Do not rush into decisions about your money. Before you take action, make sure your choice stands up to the principles outlined in The Five Laws of Gold.

And remember: A part of all you earn is yours to keep!

Lesson 5

Chapter Ten: "The Clay Tablets from Babylon"

Debt is a common problem, and it can be one of the greatest obstacles to creating wealth. Most people find themselves in debt to some degree at some point in their lives—at times it may seem overwhelming. But eliminating debt is, in most cases, the first step toward financial independence. The clay tablets in Chapter Ten describe a practical strategy for eliminating debt, and demonstrate the value of getting started today.

This lesson, like the others, will help you apply those strategies to lay a solid foundation for your future. But the lessons you'll learn here go well beyond debt reduction alone. The good habits and discipline you'll develop here will also be valuable in every other aspect of your plan to create wealth.

Questions

1. Explain the factors that helped Dabasir maintain his courage and determination to stick with his plan. What was his "why"?

2. In your own words, describe the plan's three essentials that Mathon, the gold lender, suggested to Dabasir so he could reestablish himself as a respected citizen of Babylon.

3. Did Mathon's plan take into consideration the natural human desires for pleasure and enjoyment, or was it a punishment for past errors? Do you think the plan is workable without eliminating the fun in life?

4. When is the best time to implement a great plan for your future? You can't change the past, you are where you are. But you can change your direction. Will you move toward a positive future, or continuing doing what you're doing? Will it be easier to make changes now, or wait until you've traveled further down a path that doesn't take you where you want to go? Yes, the best answers are obvious, but acting on them takes commitment. Are you ready to commit to creating a better future for yourself?

5. In paying off his creditors fairly and honorably, would it have been best for Dabasir to pay an equal amount to each, or should he have paid proportionately, paying more against the higher balances so each creditor would be paid off at the same time? Which way would be more fair?

6. Some strategists advise people who owe balances on several credit cards or loans to pay the minimum payment on each debt, except for the one with the lowest balance. On that account, they say, you should pay the minimum balance plus any leftover amount budgeted for debt repayment. That way, as the thinking goes, you will pay that account off faster, and you can then pay a larger amount against the next lowest balance. Do you believe that's a sound strategy? Why or why not?

7. Do you feel Dabasir was fundamentally honest and had never wanted to avoid his debts? If so, why hadn't he tried sooner to pay them?

8. In Dabasir's story, debt was his greatest obstacle. What things did he have to learn about himself, his spending habits, and the future he'd face if he continued on his current course, before he could overcome that obstacle?

9. Each of Dabasir's creditors responded differently to his proposed plan for repayment. Do you think his past influenced their attitude? Would a man who had gone into debt because of misfortunes beyond his control—rather than his own indiscretions—been afforded more courtesy and accommodation?

10. When his business slowed and his earnings shrank painfully, how did Dabasir get by? Did he incur more debt to maintain his standard of living? Do you feel the way Dabasir and his wife handled their setback was justified and wise?

11. Considering how critical many of Dabasir's creditors were at first, can you explain the surprising change in attitude when Dabasir made the last payments? Why would a tightwad like Alkahad offer to loan him money again, after their history?

12. Dabasir didn't have a regular income to rely upon, while Professor Shrewsbury did. Which circumstance made it easier to implement and sustain the repayment plan? Why?

13. Before Professor Shrewsbury adopted Mathon's plan, his efforts to live within his means and get out of debt had been in vain. He described it as a "downward spiral." Why do you think Mathon's plan helped Shrewsbury break the downward debt spiral, when he'd been unable to do it before?

14. What benefits could Shrewsbury offer the merchants to persuade them to accept his repayment plan? Would any of them have been better off if they had refused to accept smaller payments than they'd asked for, extended over a longer period of time?

15. Do you think the determination to live on 70% of their income cost Professor Shrewsbury and his wife severe discomfort? Did it affect their mental or physical well-being? If so, in what way? Did it humiliate them? Can you envision how devising a similar plan for yourself could be seen as an interesting experiment to work out, or like solving an intriguing puzzle?

16. Professor Shrewsbury needed an account where he could manage his money similarly to the way Dabasir did, to make it easy to prioritize putting money into his own savings account, then paying back his creditors, and spending only what was left. What would it take for you to do something similar?

    A good starting place would be to arrange for direct deposit of your paycheck into your bank account, if your employer allows that. If not, just make sure you deposit all of your paycheck (or paychecks, if you're self-employed or have more than one job) into your primary account. Then, set up an automatic transfer of 10% of each deposit into a special savings account that you set up for that purpose. (Most banks and credit unions have the ability to do that for you.) From the amount that remains you can make regular payments on your debt, and use what's left for routine spending.

If you have a bank, credit union, or other financial institution you're already happy with, talk to them about how they can set up your account according to this plan. If not, talk to friends who manage their money well about any local institution they recommend, or research the policies at established banks and credit unions. Look for one that offers a free checking account, charges no fees to take money out or move it between accounts, and that pays interest on money market and savings accounts—and ideally on checking accounts as well. Of course, you'll want to make sure your money is safe, so consider only those institutions that are insured by FDIC or NCUA.

17. Once you have your accounts in place, you'll be ready to take the first steps toward building your wealth and getting out of debt just like Dabasir and Professor Shrewsbury did. Write out a detailed plan for how you'll manage the money in your new accounts. How much will you pay on each of your debts each month? Create a budget for yourself that's consistent with Mathon's plan. Allow for your necessities, such as shelter, food,

clothing—and yes, you need some recreation, too—but reserve the proper amount to pay off your debts. Do you see a way to create a plan that covers all those things?

18. After the professor and his wife paid off their debts, what did they do with the 20% of their income they had been using for debt elimination? Would that also be a good plan for you once you are free of debt? Can you improve on it in a way that would make more sense for your situation?

19. When considering this lesson in its broadest sense, what is the most important requirement to succeed in overcoming obstacles? If you feel there are several requirements of equal importance, name them and explain your reasons.

You have now completed your work in this Study Guide, but I hope you will not close the book on your learning. As you continue your lifelong study of this and many other great books, I'll leave you with two quotes from Jim Rohn, one of my favorite authors.

> "Formal education will make you a living;
> self-education will make you a fortune."

> "You're where you are in life primarily for three reasons:
> the books you've read, the people you know,
> and your philosophies of life."

Happy reading.

GEORGE S. CLASON was born in Louisiana, Missouri, on November 7, 1874, and died on April 7, 1957. He was founder of the Clason Publishing Company and the Clason Map Company, which published the first road atlas of the United States and Canada. In 1926 he began to publish a series of pamphlets with stories set in ancient Babylon, describing strategies for thrift and financial success. These pamphlets were widely distributed by banks and insurance companies and became familiar to millions. The most famous story was called "The Richest Man in Babylon." The pamphlets were later compiled into a single book under that title, and ultimately became a classic in the study of personal finance.

RANDY L. THURMAN, CFP®, CPA/PFS, graduated from college with two degrees and a complete lack of understanding of personal finance. After losing his life savings to a stockbroker in 1985, he became obsessed with a desire to learn how an average person can become financially independent (and avoid mistakes like the one he made). He read every book he could find on the subject, and George Clason's original edition of *The Richest Man in Babylon* was one of the first. Randy took classes in personal finance and investing, acquired his CFP® and CPA designations, and started his career as a financial advisor in 1986. He never looked back. In 1990 he founded his firm, The Financial Planning Company of Oklahoma, which in 1997 merged with Retirement Investment Advisors, Inc. He continues today as Chief Executive Officer. As of this writing, Randy or his firm have been cited more than 38 times in national publications as among the best in the United States.

Made in the USA
Coppell, TX
01 June 2025